Probability
and Chi-Square
for
Biology Students

Second Edition

Sandra F. Cooper
Thomas R. Mertens
Ball State University

EMI EDUCATIONAL METHODS / CHICAGO
A DIVISION OF DEVELOPMENT SYSTEMS CORPORATION

We are indebted to the Literary Executor of the late Sir Ronald A. Fisher, F.R.S., Cambridge, to Dr. Frank Yates, F.R.S., Rothamsted, and to Messrs. Oliver and Boyd Ltd., Edinburgh, for permission to reprint Table III from their book *Statistical Tables for Biological, Agricultural and Medical Research.*

Contents

TO THE STUDENT   v

HOW TO USE THIS BOOK   ix

I.   BASIC PROBABILITY PRINCIPLES   1
     Section 1: Possibility   2
     Section 2: Probability of Simultaneous
                 Events—Multiply   16
     Section 3: Either-Or—Add   32
     Progress Quiz   39

II. BINOMIAL EXPANSION   42
     Section 1: Expanding the Binomial   43
     Progress Quiz   68
     Section 2: The Binomial Expansion Principle,
                 Calculating Probabilities and
                 Solving Genetics Problems   70
     Progress Quiz   75

III. THE CHI-SQUARE TEST   77
      Progress Quiz   94

IV. COMPREHENSIVE REVIEW   98

APPENDIX A
     Table of Chi-Square Values   108

APPENDIX B
     Answers to Progress Quizzes   112

BIBLIOGRAPHY   117

To the Student

An appreciation of fundamental concepts of probability is basic to understanding a number of scientific disciplines. Various biological sciences, such as genetics and ecology, make use of these concepts and simple statistical tests such as the chi-square test. For example, probability considerations are essential to the basic laws of heredity developed by Gregor Mendel and the classical transmission geneticists of the early twentieth century. Furthermore, the chi-square test is a tool used in analyzing the data obtained in genetics crosses and other types of biological investigations. You will not progress very far in the study of biology before you encounter the need for the basic concepts of probability and chi-square.

Many science students, and perhaps most biology students, encounter some need for formal instruction in these basic principles. This book has been designed to assist you in obtaining such instruction. It has been written in an inductive fashion, leading you from specific examples and facts to broad principles and generalizations. The authors have purposely not given you "rules" to follow, but they have provided you with meaningful examples that should enable you to determine the rules that apply to the various situations discussed. This approach should insure that generalizations, once made, are meaningful to you.

Probability and Chi-Square is different from most books you have read. It is a programed text. It consists of appropriate background information followed by a series of questions and problems which you are to answer. The answers to the questions and problems are also provided, and great care has been taken to outline the reasoning process underlying the answers given.

You will find this book most helpful if you are just beginning to learn about probability and chi-square. On the other hand, if you are experienced in these matters, you will find that the book will provide you with a suitable summary and review of familiar material. The more knowledgeable student will find the content of the book sufficiently sophisticated to be challenging, while the beginning student will find it structured enough to lead him, step-by-step, to an understanding of important concepts.

A knowledge of basic Mendelian genetics and elementary algebra will be helpful to you when studying this program. If you need review, we suggest you consult appropriate high school or college textbooks dealing with these topics before you get too far along with your study of the program.

Because of the program's organization, you must progress through it from the beginning to the end. You cannot skip around and retain the meaningful structure of the book. Rather, you should progress through the program at the speed necessary for you. Parts of the book may be more readily comprehended than others; you should vary your study speed to fit the level of difficulty of the material with which you are dealing. Progress quizzes at appropriate places in the program will enable you to test your comprehension of the material you have been studying.

Student Verification

You can be sure this book works because all books in the Educational Methods Programed Biology Series (PBS) have been tested in classrooms across the country with students like yourself. All of the PBS books have been tested and revised with you in mind. We want you to be able to use our books with confidence. This process of testing and revising our books in accordance with student performance and comments insures you quality products that *work*. Students who tested this program were competent in the performances listed at the right, after the program's completion. (Statistical data is available upon request.)

Performance Objectives—Competency Statements

After you've conscientiously studied this book, you will be able to:

- determine the number of possible ways in which a series of separate events can occur;

- determine the number of possible ways in which a series of several possibilities will occur;

- determine the probability of the simultaneous occurrence of two or more independent events;

- determine the probability of the occurrence of either one or the other of two or more separate events;

- expand the binomial $(a + b)^N$ and use the expanded binomial in calculating probabilities;

- calculate and interpret chi-square in determining the goodness-of-fit of data to a particular hypothesized ratio.

Performance Objectives or *Competency Statements* are given at the beginning of each chapter. Use them as a guide. They will tell you what you will be expected to do at the completion of that chapter.

How to Use This Book

This may be a new type of instructional book for you. Its subject matter has been broken down into a series of numbered frames. The subject matter has been organized (programed) in such a way that the book will be self-instructional. Using this book you can teach yourself the fundamentals of probability and chi-square. Each frame in the program builds on information you have learned in preceding frames. For that reason it is important that you do not skip around in the program. The sequence of the frames is important and is designed to help you learn more efficiently.

Respond at Every Frame

Some frames present new information; others review material presented earlier; many of the frames consist of problems to be solved using the information developed in preceding frames. Every frame presents a learning situation requiring you to respond. You may be asked to make one of the following types of responses:

- write an answer in a blank space;

- answer a question in one or two words;

- write a sentence, phrase or clause in answer to a question;

- choose the correct answer from several alternatives;

- solve a problem.

You must make the calculations necessary to solve the problems, and write your answers. Once you have written your answer, you will want to find out whether you have responded correctly. Programed instruction provides you with immediate feedback by giving you the answers to the questions asked. The answers are separated from each question by a single line. The immediate feedback is an important part of the learning process and will enable you to readily determine how your learning is progressing. *Do not look at the correct answer until after you have made the necessary calculations and recorded your own answer.* If you look before answering, you will only impair your own learning.

Use an Answer Mask

To avoid seeing the correct answer inadvertently before recording your own answer, make an Answer Mask by folding an $8\frac{1}{2}$" x 11" piece of paper in half.

1. As you start a page, cover it with the Answer Mask.

2. Slide the mask down until you see the heavy horizontal line that runs across the entire page. This line separates each frame from its correct answer.

3. When you reach the horizontal line, stop moving the mask. Read the frame carefully; then, record your answer. Make sure you write each answer; in those problems involving calculations show the steps you used in reaching the answer. Do *not* simply think the answer and then go on. Considerably more learning will be accomplished by actually making the calculations and writing your answer.

4. Slide the mask down to reveal the correct answer. If the frame which you are studying contains several parts, such as a, b and c, you may reveal the answer to each part before proceeding to the next part of the frame.

5. If your answer was correct, move the mask down to the next heavy horizontal line and proceed with the new frame you have just uncovered.

6. If your answer was wrong, go back, restudy the frame (and, if necessary, restudy several preceding frames) until you understand your error and know why the

answer given is correct. Then proceed to the next frame. (Note that in the answers to the frames, care has been taken to show the reasoning process you must employ in arriving at the correct answer.)

Progress Quizzes and Comprehensive Review

Four progress quizzes are included at appropriate places in this book. Each quiz will help you and your instructor to evaluate how well you have mastered the material covered. Answers to the quizzes are provided in Appendix B at the end of the book. Refer to the answers only after you have completed an entire progress quiz.

The comprehensive review at the end of the book serves as a summary of the entire program. Problems representative of each of the major parts of the book are included in this review. You must be able to solve the problems in the review if you are to complete the final examination successfully.

I
BASIC
PROBABILITY
PRINCIPLES

Performance Objectives

As a result of conscientious study of this chapter, you will be able to

- determine the number of possible ways in which a series of separate events can occur;

- determine the probability that one particular event among several possibilities will occur;

- determine the probability of the simultaneous occurrence of two or more independent events;

- determine the probability of the occurrence of either one or the other of two or more separate events;

- apply basic probability principles to solving simple problems having to do with biological systems—especially in the fields of genetics, ecology and the structure of biological molecules;

- complete rules applying to basic probability.

Section 1: Possibility

1.   To deal with probabilities, you must first determine all of the possibilities, or alternative ways in which an event can happen. In tossing a coin, for example, there are two possibilities, heads or tails. For a six-sided die there are six possibilities or alternatives, since any one of the six sides may be turned face up. From a 52-card deck of cards, how many alternatives are there? In other words, any one of how many possible cards may be drawn from such a deck? _____

52; If you draw only one card, it could be any one of the 52 cards in the deck.

2.   A coin is flipped into the air. It can land on either side. In this example, how many possible ways are there in which the coin may land? _____

2

3.   Two coins are flipped into the air simultaneously.

a.   Coin 1 has how many possibilities? _____
b.   Coin 2 has how many possibilities? _____
c.   The two coins *together* have how many possibilities? _____

---

a.   Coin 1 has two possibilities—head (H) or tail(T).

b.   Coin 2 has two possibilities—H or T.

c.   Coins 1 *and* 2 together have four possibilities. (The possibilities for each are multiplied together; 2 × 2 = 4 possibilities.)

4.   If two coins are flipped into the air simultaneously, what are the four possible combinations for the two coins?

Write H or T in each blank in the chart below to obtain the four different combinations.

Possibilities for Coin 1

	H	T
H	HH	
T		

Possibilities for Coin 2

Possibilities for Coin 1

	H	B
H	HH	(HT)
T	(TH)	TT

Possibilities for Coin 2

Note in the checkerboard that there can be HT or TH. Therefore,

3

there are two possible ways of getting a head *and* a tail. It might be argued by some that there are only three possibilities for both coins (i.e., two heads, two tails, or a head and a tail), HT and TH each being "a head and a tail." However, if we designate the order, such as $H_1 T_2$ (heads for Coin 1, tails for Coin 2) then we have four different possibilities; i.e., $2 \times 2 = 4$.

5.   A boy and a girl, both students in biology, take an examination. Each of them can get either a passing or a failing grade on the examination.

a.   How many possibilities are there with respect to passing or failing for each student taking the examination? _____
b.   How many possible combinations of passing or failing grades are there for the boy and girl *together?* _____

---

a.   There are two possibilities for each student—pass or fail.

b.

Boy		Girl		Possible Grade Combinations for Boy and Girl
2	X	2	=	4

6.   A boy and a girl take an examination. Each can either pass or fail the examination. Considering the two students together, there are four possible combinations of grades for them. What are these combinations? Fill in the chart, including the headings.

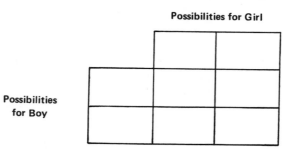

Possibilities for Girl

Possibilities for Boy

Possibilities for Girl

	P	F
P	PP	PF
F	FP	FF

Possibilities for Boy

7.   Suppose letter grades are given on the next biology examination. Each of the two students can score an A, B, C, D or F.

a.   How many possible grades can the boy earn? _____
b.   How many possible grades can the girl earn? _____
c.   How many possible grade combinations are there for the boy and the girl?   _____
d.   Show all the possible grade combinations for the boy and the girl.

Possibilities for Girl

	A	B	C	D	F
A					
B					
C					
D					
F					

Possibilities for Boy

a. The boy can earn five possible grades—A, B, C, D or F.
b. The girl can also earn five possible grades—A, B, C, D or F.
c. For the boy *and* girl there are 25 possible combinations (5 X 5).
d. The possible grade combinations for the boy and the girl are:

Possibilities for Girl

		A	B	C	D	F
	A	AA	AB	AC	AD	AF
	B	BA	BB	BC	BD	BF
Possibilities for Boy	C	CA	CB	CC	CD	CF
	D	DA	DB	DC	DD	DF
	F	FA	FB	FC	FD	FF

8. A pair of dice is rolled. One die is white, the other red. Each die has six faces.

a. In how many possible ways can the white die fall? _____
b. In how many possible ways can the red die fall? _____
c. How many possible combinations are there for the red die and white die? _____

a. There are six possibilities for the white die (a cube has six faces).

6

b. There are six possibilities for the red die.

c. There are 36 possibilities for the red die *and* white die together.

White		Red		Possible Combinations
6	X	6	=	36

9. A deck of playing cards consists of four suits—hearts, clubs, spades and diamonds. Each suit contains 13 cards, two through ten plus a jack, a queen, a king and an ace.

a. If you draw any card from the 52-card deck, how many different possible cards could you draw? _____

b. If you draw a heart from the deck, how many different possible hearts could you draw? _____

c. If you draw a five from the deck, how many different fives are possible? _____

---

a. 52

b. 13

c. four, since there are four suits

10. Two cards are drawn from a deck of 52 cards. The first card, a five, could belong to any one of the four suits. The second card, a seven, could belong to any one of the four suits. Therefore, there are how many possible combinations of suits for the two cards? _____

The first card can be a five from any of the four suits—hearts, clubs, spades or diamonds. Therefore, there are four possibilities for the first card. The same is true of the second card. So,

Card 1		Card 2		Possible Combinations
4	X	4	=	16

11. In beans, two pairs of genes are concerned with two different seed characteristics. The phenotype or appearance of the bean is controlled by these genes. One gene pair controls whether the seed has a smooth or wrinkled texture. The other gene pair controls whether the seed is circular or oval in shape.

a. How many different phenotypes are there concerning seed texture? _____

b. How many different phenotypes are there concerning seed shape? _____

c. How many possible combinations of these two characteristics are there? _____

d. What are the various phenotypic combinations?

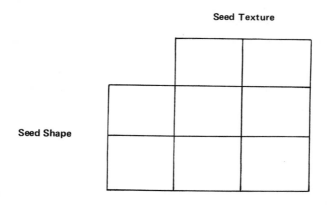

a. There are two possibilities concerning seed texture—smooth or wrinkled.

b. There are two possibilities concerning seed shape—circular or oval.

c. There are four possible phenotypic combinations.

Seed Texture		Seed Shape		
2	X	2	=	4

d. The possible phenotypic combinations are:

Seed Texture

	smooth	wrinkled
oval	oval smooth	oval wrinkled
circular	circular smooth	circular wrinkled

Seed Shape

12. In living organisms there are 20 different commonly occurring amino acids. A *di*peptide is made up of *two* amino acids.

a. There are how many possible amino acids for the first amino acid in a dipeptide? _____
b. There are how many possible amino acids for the second amino acid in a dipeptide? _____
c. There are how many possible dipeptides? _____

---

a. For the first amino acid in the dipeptide there are 20 possible amino acids.
b. There are also 20 possibilities for the second amino acid in the dipeptide.
c. Therefore, there are 400 different dipeptides possible (20 X 20).

First Amino Acid		Second Amino Acid		Dipeptides
20	X	20	=	400

9

13. A student was given an unknown dipeptide. In the laboratory he eliminated, for the first amino acid, 15 of the 20 possible amino acids; for the second amino acid, he eliminated all except three. How many combinations of amino acids are possible for his unknown dipeptide?

First Amino Acid		Second Amino Acid		Possible Dipeptides
5	X	3	=	15

14. We are now prepared to formulate a generalization or principle. *If one event can happen in "a" number of ways and a second event, occurring simultaneously and being independent of the first event, can happen in "b" number of ways, then the two events together can occur in "a" times "b" number of ways, or the product of the possibilities for each separate event.*

In other words, when two events occur, the number of possibilities for both occurring together is: (Check one letter.)

_____ a.   the number of possibilities for the first event added to the number of possibilities for the second event.
_____ b.   the number of possibilities for the first event multiplied by the number of possibilities for the second event.

For this to occur, the two events must be: (Check one.)
_____ c.   dependent on each other.
_____ d.   independent of each other.

---

b.   the number of possibilities for the first event multiplied by the number of possibilities for the second event.
d.   independent of each other.

10

15. This principle can be extended to determine the number of possibilities for three or more independently occurring events.

There are three students who take an examination and each student can pass or fail.

a. With respect to passing or failing, how many possibilities are there for each student? _____
b. How many possibilities are there for all three students? _____
c. List all possible combinations for the three students.

---

a. There are two possibilities for each student — passing or failing.
b. For all three students, there are:

Student 1		Student 2		Student 3		All Three
2	X	2	X	2	=	2^3 or 8

c. The possible combinations for the three students are:

1. P P P	3. P F P	5. F F P	7. P F F
2. P P F	4. F P P	6. F P F	8. F F F

16. Tripeptides are made of *three* amino acids. Remembering that there are 20 different amino acids which commonly occur in natural proteins, how many different possible tripeptides are there? _____

Amino Acid 1		Amino Acid 2		Amino Acid 3		Possible Tripeptides
20	X	20	X	20	=	20^3 or 8,000

17. How many different tripeptides are possible if the middle amino acid in the tripeptide is alanine? _____

Amino Acid 1		Amino Acid 2		Amino Acid 3		Possible Tripeptides
20	X	1	X	20	=	400

18. In a family of three children,

a. How many possibilities are there for the sex of the first child? _____
b. How many possibilities are there for the sex of the second child? _____
c. The third child? _____

a. For the first child, there are two possibilities—male or female.
b. Two—male or female.
c. Two—male or female.

19. In a family of three children,

a. How many different combinations of boys and girls are possible? _____

12

b. List these possible combinations.

---

a. **Child 1**   **Child 2**   **Child 3**   **Family**

   2   X   2   X   2   = 2^3 or 8

b. The different combinations of boys and girls in a family of three children are:

   1. B B B   3. B G B   5. G G B   7. B G G
   2. B B G   4. G B B   6. G B G   8. G G G

20. There are four nitrogen-containing bases found in the deoxyribonucleic acid (DNA) molecule. They are adenine, guanine, cytosine and thymine.

a. For a four-base sequence, such as GCTA, CAGG or AAAA, and so on, how many possible combinations are there? _____
b. For a three-base sequence, such as CTG, TTT or ACG, and so on, how many possible combinations are there? _____

---

a. **Base 1**   **Base 2**   **Base 3**   **Base 4**   **Four-Base Sequence**

   4   X   4   X   4   X   4   = 4^4 or 256

b. **Base 1**   **Base 2**   **Base 3**   **Three-Base Sequence**

   4   X   4   X   4   = 4^3 or 64

13

21. A female has the genotype *AaBb*. A capital and small letter stand for two variations of the same trait.

a. How many different kinds of gametes can she produce? _____
b. What are they?

---

a.

Trait A		Trait B		Gametic Possibilities
2 possibilities (*A* and *a*)	X	2 possibilities (*B* and *b*)	=	4

b. Female gametic possibilities: *AB, Ab, aB, ab.*

22. A male has the genotype *AABb*.

a. How many different kinds of gametes can he produce? _____
b. What are they?

---

a.

Trait A		Trait B		Gametic Possibilities
1 possibility (*A*)	X	2 possibilities (*B* and *b*)	=	2

b. Male gametic possibilities: *AB, Ab.*

23. A female has the genotype *AaBb* and a male has the genotype *AABb*.

a. How many possible combinations of male and female gametes are there? _____
b. Show these possibilities in a "checkerboard" or chart. In genetics, this kind of diagram is called a Punnett Square.

---

a.

Female Gametic Possibilities	Male Gametic Possibilities	Gametic Combinations
4 X	2 =	8

b. The eight possibilities may be illustrated as follows:

Female Gametic Possibilities

	AB	Ab	aB	ab
Male Gametic Possibilities AB	AABB	AABb	AaBB	AaBb
Ab	AAbB	AAbb	AabB	Aabb

Note that not all of the eight possible combinations are different.

24. The total number of possibilities resulting from any number of independently occurring events is determined by: (Check one.)

_____ a. adding the number of possibilities for each respective event.

_____ b. multiplying the number of possibilities for each respective event.

---

b. multiplying

Section 2: Probability of Simultaneous Events—Multiply

25. Probability is the *chance* that one particular event will happen out of all the possibilities. Probability may be expressed as a fraction, a percentage or a ratio. In this book, we will usually express probability as a fraction.

If a coin is flipped,

a. In how many different ways can it land? _____
b. What chance do you have of getting a head? _____
c. What chance do you have of getting a tail? _____

---

a. A coin can land in two different ways, heads or tails.
b. The probability of a head: one chance out of two possibilities or $\frac{1}{2}$.
c. The probability of a tail: one chance out of two possibilities or $\frac{1}{2}$.

26. A deck of cards contains four aces. If you hold only the four aces in your hand, what is the probability of someone drawing the ace of diamonds from your hand?

One chance out of four possibilities or $\frac{1}{4}$.

27. From the entire deck of 52 cards, the probability of getting an ace on the first draw is _____ .

---

four chances out of 52 or $\frac{4}{52}$ or $\frac{1}{13}$

28. The probability of rolling a die and getting a three is _____ .

---

one chance out of six or $\frac{1}{6}$

29. Two dice are rolled simultaneously.

a. The probability of getting a three on the first die is _____ .
b. The probability of getting a five on the second die is _____ .
c. The probability of getting a three on the first die and a five on the second die is_____ .

a. The probability of getting a three on the first die is $\frac{1}{6}$.

b. The probability of getting a five on the second die is $\frac{1}{6}$.

c. Therefore, the probability of getting a three on the first die simultaneously with a five on the second die is $\frac{1}{6} \times \frac{1}{6}$ or $\frac{1}{36}$.

30. The probability of drawing the five of hearts from one deck of cards and, simultaneously, the ace of spades from a second deck would be _____ .

---

one chance out of 52 for each draw; therefore,

First Draw		Second Draw		Both
$\dfrac{1}{52}$	$\times$	$\dfrac{1}{52}$	$=$	$\dfrac{1}{2,704}$

31. Assuming all four nucleotides to be equally available, the probability of getting a base sequence of GATC in a chain of four nucleotides would be _____ .

The probability of getting guanine for the first base is one out of four possible bases or $\frac{1}{4}$, and the probability of getting adenine for the second base is one chance out of four possible bases or $\frac{1}{4}$, and so on. Therefore, the probability for the particular base sequence GATC is $\frac{1}{4}$ X $\frac{1}{4}$ X $\frac{1}{4}$ X $\frac{1}{4}$ or $\frac{1}{256}$.

Base 1		Base 2		Base 3		Base 4		Four-Base Sequence
$\frac{1}{4}$	X	$\frac{1}{4}$	X	$\frac{1}{4}$	X	$\frac{1}{4}$	=	$\frac{1}{256}$

32. In a family of two children,

a. What is the probability that both will be boys? _____
b. What is the probability that both will be girls? _____

The probability is $\frac{1}{2}$ that each child will be a boy and $\frac{1}{2}$ that each child will be a girl. Therefore,

		Child 1		Child 2		Both	
a.	Boys	$\frac{1}{2}$	X	$\frac{1}{2}$	=	$\frac{1}{4}$	that both will be boys
b.	Girls	$\frac{1}{2}$	X	$\frac{1}{2}$	=	$\frac{1}{4}$	that both will be girls

33. What is the *probability* that a couple would have a family of four children—two boys and two girls—and *in that order?* _____

There are two possibilities in each case, that is, for child 1 there are two possibilities—a boy or a girl; for child 2 there are two possibilities—a boy or a girl, and so on. Therefore, for child 1, the probability of having a boy is one out of two possibilities or $\frac{1}{2}$. For child 2, the probability of having a boy is also one out of two possibilities or $\frac{1}{2}$. For child 3, the probability of having a girl is one out of two or $\frac{1}{2}$, and this is also true for child 4. Following this, the probability of two boys followed by two

19

girls is:

Child 1		Child 2		Child 3		Child 4		Four Children
$\frac{1}{2}$	X	$\frac{1}{2}$	X	$\frac{1}{2}$	X	$\frac{1}{2}$	=	$\frac{1}{16}$

34. In a family of four children, two boys (B) and two girls (G), six different combinations or orders are possible. These are:

1.	B G B G		4.	G B G B
2.	G G B B		5.	B G G B
3.	B B G G		6.	G B B G

What is the probability that a couple would have two boys and two girls in *any one* of the six possible combinations? _____

The probability for any *one* of these different orders is $\frac{1}{16}$, determined as follows:

The Probability of	Child 1		Child 2		Child 3		Child 4		Four Children
BGBG	$\frac{1}{2}$	X	$\frac{1}{2}$	X	$\frac{1}{2}$	X	$\frac{1}{2}$	=	$\frac{1}{16}$
GGBB	$\frac{1}{2}$	X	$\frac{1}{2}$	X	$\frac{1}{2}$	X	$\frac{1}{2}$	=	$\frac{1}{16}$
BBGG	$\frac{1}{2}$	X	$\frac{1}{2}$	X	$\frac{1}{2}$	X	$\frac{1}{2}$	=	$\frac{1}{16}$
GBGB	$\frac{1}{2}$	X	$\frac{1}{2}$	X	$\frac{1}{2}$	X	$\frac{1}{2}$	=	$\frac{1}{16}$
BGGB	$\frac{1}{2}$	X	$\frac{1}{2}$	X	$\frac{1}{2}$	X	$\frac{1}{2}$	=	$\frac{1}{16}$
GBBG	$\frac{1}{2}$	X	$\frac{1}{2}$	X	$\frac{1}{2}$	X	$\frac{1}{2}$	=	$\frac{1}{16}$

35. A box contains a total of 100 marbles, including 25 blue marbles, 20 yellow marbles, 15 green marbles and 40 red marbles.

a. What is the probability of a blindfolded student picking a yellow marble on his first draw? _____
b. A blue marble? _____
c. A green marble? _____

---

a. The probability of getting a yellow marble would be 20 out of 100 (since there are 100 marbles in the container) or $\frac{20}{100}$ or $\frac{1}{5}$.
b. Probability of a blue marble would be $\frac{25}{100}$ or $\frac{1}{4}$.
c. Probability of a green marble would be $\frac{15}{100}$ or $\frac{3}{20}$.

36. An experiment was conducted in an attempt to determine the ability of insects to perceive and distinguish between colors. Bees were used as the experimental insects. Disks of yellow and blue were placed on beehives and the bees were observed to choose one disk or the other. Bees of three different strains were used. The following observations were made:

Selection Preference of Bees of Strain 1		Selection Preference of Bees of Strain 2		Selection Preference of Bees of Strain 3	
Yellow	Blue	Yellow	Blue	Yellow	Blue
$\frac{4}{5}$	$\frac{1}{5}$	$\frac{2}{3}$	$\frac{1}{3}$	$\frac{1}{2}$	$\frac{1}{2}$

A bee from strain 1 was observed to choose the yellow disk $\frac{4}{5}$ of the time, a bee of strain 2 chose the yellow disk $\frac{2}{3}$ of the time and a bee from strain 3 chose the yellow disk $\frac{1}{2}$ of the time. Assuming the choices to be independent of each other,

a. What is the probability of bees of strains 1, 2 and 3 all choosing yellow? _____

b. Of strains 1 and 2 choosing yellow and strain 3 choosing blue (YYB)? _____

c. Of BBY? _____

d. Of BBB? _____

	Strain 1		Strain 2		Strain 3			
a.	$\frac{4}{5}$	X	$\frac{2}{3}$	X	$\frac{1}{2}$	=	$\frac{8}{30}$ or	$\frac{4}{15}$
b.	$\frac{4}{5}$	X	$\frac{2}{3}$	X	$\frac{1}{2}$	=	$\frac{8}{30}$ or	$\frac{4}{15}$
c.	$\frac{1}{5}$	X	$\frac{1}{3}$	X	$\frac{1}{2}$	=	$\frac{1}{30}$	
d.	$\frac{1}{5}$	X	$\frac{1}{3}$	X	$\frac{1}{2}$	=	$\frac{1}{30}$	

37. The gene for albinism (a) is recessive to the gene for normal pigmentation (A) in human beings. If two individuals, both of whom are heterozygous (Aa) for the albino characteristic, are mated,

a. How many kinds of gametes can each parent produce? _____

b. How many possible combinations of these gametes are there? _____

c. What are these possible combinations?

Female

Male

d.   What is the probability of an albino being born to parents, both of whom are heterozygous for the albino characteristic?

_____

---

a.   Since the parents are both heterozygous, their gametes can contain either gene A (normal) or gene a (albinism). Therefore, each parent produces two types of gametes concerning albinism— A and a.

b.   The number of possible combinations of these are:

Male Gametes		Female Gametes		Zygotic Combinations
2	X	2	=	4

c.   There are four combinations.

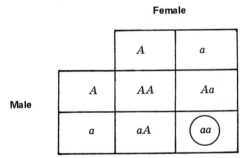

Female

	A	a
A	AA	Aa
a	aA	aa

Male

d.   Therefore, the probability of an albino being born to parents heterozygous for this trait is one out of four or $\frac{1}{4}$.

38.   Two individuals are heterozygous for the albino characteristic.

a.   What is the probability of their having an albino child? _____
b.   What is the probability of their having a boy? _____
c.   What is the probability of their having an albino boy? _____

a. Probability of an albino is $\frac{1}{4}$ (see frame 37).
b. Probability of a boy is $\frac{1}{2}$.
c.

Probability of an Albino		Probability of a Boy		Probability of an Albino Boy
$\frac{1}{4}$	X	$\frac{1}{2}$	=	$\frac{1}{8}$

39. A man and his wife are each known to be heterozygous for the albino characteristic.

a. What is the probability of their having four consecutive albino offspring? _____
b. What is the probability of their having a boy? _____
c. A girl? _____
d. What is the probability of their having four consecutive albinos, the first a boy, followed by three girls? _____

Probability of

First Albino		Second Albino		Third Albino		Fourth Albino		Four Consecutive Albinos

$$\frac{1}{4} \quad \times \quad \frac{1}{4} \quad \times \quad \frac{1}{4} \quad \times \quad \frac{1}{4} \quad = \quad \frac{1}{256}$$

b. The probability of having a boy is $\frac{1}{2}$.

c. Likewise, the probability of a girl is $\frac{1}{2}$.

d.

Probability of

Four Consecutive Albinos		Boy		Girl		Girl		Girl		Four Consecutive Albinos, First a Boy, Then Three Girls

$$\frac{1}{256} \quad \times \quad \frac{1}{2} \quad \times \quad \frac{1}{2} \quad \times \quad \frac{1}{2} \quad \times \quad \frac{1}{2} \quad = \quad \frac{1}{4,096}$$

Or this could be worked out a second way:

Probability of

First Child Being Albino		First Child Being a Boy		An Albino Boy

$$\frac{1}{4} \quad \times \quad \frac{1}{2} \quad = \quad \frac{1}{8}$$

Second Child Being Albino		Second Child Being a Girl		An Albino Girl

$$\frac{1}{4} \quad \times \quad \frac{1}{2} \quad = \quad \frac{1}{8}$$

Third Child Being Albino		Third Child Being a Girl		An Albino Girl

$$\frac{1}{4} \quad \times \quad \frac{1}{2} \quad = \quad \frac{1}{8}$$

Fourth Child Being Albino		Fourth Child Being a Girl		An Albino Girl

$$\frac{1}{4} \quad \times \quad \frac{1}{2} \quad = \quad \frac{1}{8}$$

$$\frac{1}{8} \times \frac{1}{8} \times \frac{1}{8} \times \frac{1}{8} = \frac{1}{4,096}$$

25

40. Remembering that the probability of heterozygous parents having an albino child is $\frac{1}{4}$,

a. What is the probability of their having a normal child? _____
b. Four consecutive normal children? _____

---

a. Three of the four possible types of offspring would be normal (AA, Aa, aA). Therefore, the probability of heterozygous parents having a child with the normal pigmentation is three chances out of four or $\frac{3}{4}$.

b. $\frac{3}{4} \times \frac{3}{4} \times \frac{3}{4} \times \frac{3}{4} = \frac{81}{256}$

41. Briefly, in blood type inheritance, the gene for type O may be considered recessive and the genes for A and B may be considered as dominant to gene O, but co-dominant with respect to each other.

a. If an individual receives the gene for type O blood from one parent and the gene for type B blood from the other parent, the individual will have what blood type? _____
b. If an individual receives the gene for type O blood from one parent and the gene for type A blood from the other parent, the individual will have what blood type? _____
c. If each parent contributes a gene for type O blood to their offspring, the offspring will have what blood type? _____
d. If one parent contributes a gene for type A blood and the offspring has type AB blood, the second parent must have contributed a gene for what blood type? _____

a. Type *B*, because the gene for type *B* blood is dominant to the gene for type *O* blood.
b. Type *A*, because the gene for type *A* is dominant to the gene for type *O* blood.
c. Type *O*—the genotype is *OO*, therefore, the recessive genes are expressed.
d. *B*, because both genes, *A* and *B*, are present in the type *AB* offspring and each is expressed equally; that is, *A* and *B* are co-dominant with respect to each other.

42. A man having blood type *A*, whose mother was type *O*, marries a woman having type *AB* blood.

a. What are the possible blood types for their children?
_____

b. What is the probability of their having children with type *A* blood? _____

a.

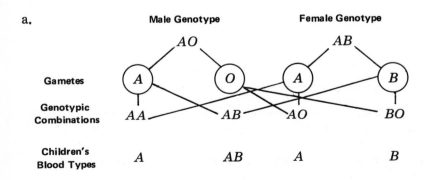

27

b. There are two chances out of four for blood type $A-\frac{2}{4}$ or $\frac{1}{2}$.

43. Generation I

Generation II

Generation III

○ = Female
□ = Male

In the human pedigree diagramed above, the blood type is shown under each individual where it is known.

a. What is the probability of the female in the second generation having type A blood? _____
b. Type B blood? _____
c. What is the probability of the male in the third generation having type A blood? _____
d. Type B blood? _____
e. Type AB blood? _____
f. Type O blood? _____

Female Genotype   Male Genotype

AB   AO

B   A   O   A   Gametes

a. There are two possible genotypes for the second generation female—AO or BO. Therefore, the probability that she will have type A blood is $\frac{1}{2}$.
b. Likewise, the probability of the second generation female having type B blood is also $\frac{1}{2}$.

c.   For the third generation male, there are three possibilities, depending on the blood type of his mother. She can be type A or type B, but in each case her genotype carries the recessive O gene (since her mother was blood type O). She can contribute an A or O gene, or a B or O gene, to her son. Therefore, the probability of the second generation female having the gene for type A is $\frac{1}{2}$. The probability that if she is type A she will transmit the A gene is $\frac{1}{2}$. Since $\frac{1}{2} \times \frac{1}{2} = \frac{1}{4}$, the probability of the third generation male being type A is $\frac{1}{4}$. The second generation male has type O blood, so he can transmit only the gene for type O blood. Therefore, the probability of the third generation male having type A blood depends entirely upon the gene transmitted to him by his mother.

d.   The probability of the third generation male being type B is $\frac{1}{4}$. (See explanation for part c.)

e.   The probability of the third generation male having type AB blood is $\frac{0}{4}$—no chance—because his father has type O blood and must contribute one O gene to his son's genotype.

f.   The probability of type O blood for the third generation male is $\frac{1}{2}$. The probability that his mother passes on the O gene is $\frac{1}{2}$, whether she is A or B type. The father is certain to pass on the O gene; therefore, $\frac{1}{2} \times 1 = \frac{1}{2}$.

44.   As a result of his work with garden peas, Mendel proposed what are now recognized as the basic principles of genetics, one of which is as follows: The "hereditary factors" (now called genes) are segregated independently of each other into the gametes.

Garden peas have seven pairs of chromosomes. Mendel was fortunate, indeed, to have selected for his work seven different traits, each of which was carried on a different one of the seven chromosome pairs. What would be the probability of selecting seven traits at random in the garden pea, each trait being carried on a different one of the seven chromosome pairs? _____

About $\frac{1}{163}$ (See next two frames for explanation.)

45. As given in frame 44, the first gene can be on any chromosome pair of the seven. Therefore, the probability of the allele for the first trait being on one of the seven pairs of chromosomes is $\frac{7}{7}$ or 1.

The allele for the second trait can be carried on any one of the remaining six chromosome pairs and the probability of its being on one of the remaining six (out of a total of seven) is $\frac{6}{7}$.

The allele for the third trait can be carried on any of the remaining (a.) _____ pairs of chromosomes out of a total of (b.)_____ pairs. The probability of this occurring is (c.) _____ .

The allele for the fourth trait can be carried on any of the remaining (d.) _____ pairs of chromosomes; the probability of this occurring is (e.) _____ .

The allele for the fifth trait can be carried on any of the remaining (f.)_____ pairs of chromosomes; the probability for this occurring is (g.)_____ .

The allele for the sixth trait can be carried on either of the remaining (h.) _____ pairs of chromosomes; the probability of this occuring is (i.)_____ .

The allele for the seventh trait must be carried on the (j.) _____ remaining pair of chromosomes. The probability of this occurring is (k.) _____ .

---

a. 5   d. 4   g. $\frac{3}{7}$ j. 1

b. 7   e. $\frac{4}{7}$ h. 2   k. $\frac{1}{7}$

c. $\frac{5}{7}$ f. 3   i. $\frac{2}{7}$

46. By using the individual probabilities for each separate trait being carried on a different chromosome, we (multiply/divide) _____ the separate probabilities of the individual events to arrive at the probability of their occurring simultaneously.

Therefore, for the garden pea, the probability of randomly selecting seven different traits, each one of which is carried on a different pair of chromosomes, is _____ X _____ X_____ X_____ X _____ X_____X_____ or_____ .

---

multiply

$$\frac{7}{7} \times \frac{6}{7} \times \frac{5}{7} \times \frac{4}{7} \times \frac{3}{7} \times \frac{2}{7} \times \frac{1}{7} = \frac{5,040}{823,543} = \frac{720}{117,649}$$

or about $\frac{1}{163}$

47. The principle or generalization concerning the probability of two simultaneously occurring independent events is:

The probability of two independent events occurring simultaneously is equal to the probability of the first event (times/plus) _____ *the probability of the second event.*

---

times

48. Would the above principle apply to the probability of three or more independent events occurring simultaneously? _____

Yes (See previous frames, especially frames 44-46.)

Section 3: Either-Or—Add

49. Suppose that you are holding two cards—the king and queen of clubs—in your hand, and one of the cards is drawn.

a. What is the probability that the queen of clubs will be drawn? _____

b. What is the probability that the king of clubs will be drawn? _____

c. What is the probability of drawing either the king or the queen of clubs? _____

---

a. The probability that the queen will be drawn is $\frac{1}{2}$.

b. The probability that the king will be drawn is $\frac{1}{2}$.

c. The probability of drawing either the king or the queen is $\frac{1}{2} + \frac{1}{2}$ or 1. Obviously, there is a 100% probability of one or the other of these two cards being drawn.

50. a. The probability of rolling a die and getting a two is _____.

b. The probability of rolling a die and getting a six is _____.

c. The probability of rolling a die and getting *either* a two *or* a six is _____.

---

a. The probability of getting a two is $\frac{1}{6}$.

b. The probability of getting a six is $\frac{1}{6}$.

c. The probability of getting either a two or a six is $\frac{1}{6} + \frac{1}{6}$ or $\frac{2}{6}$ or $\frac{1}{3}$.

51. If a card is drawn from a deck of 52 cards, what is the proba-

bility of drawing either a heart or a club? _____

The probability of drawing a heart is $\frac{13}{52}$ or $\frac{1}{4}$.

The probability of drawing a club is $\frac{13}{52}$ or $\frac{1}{4}$.

Therefore, the probability of drawing *either* a heart *or* a club is $\frac{13}{52} + \frac{13}{52}$ or $\frac{26}{52}$ or $\frac{1}{2}$.

52. Suppose that there are ten boxes of breakfast cereal on a store counter. There are prizes in three of the ten boxes—a toy soldier in one, a ring in another and a stick of gum in a third.

a.   What is the probability of getting a box with a prize? _____
b.   The box with the ring? _____
c.   Either the ring or the toy soldier? _____

---

a.   three chances in ten = $\frac{3}{10}$ = probability of getting a prize
b.   one chance in ten = $\frac{1}{10}$ = probability of getting the ring
c. $\frac{1}{10} + \frac{1}{10} = \frac{2}{10} = \frac{1}{5}$ = probability of getting either the ring or the soldier

53. Some marbles are put into a box. There are four different colors of marbles; some are yellow, some green, some blue and some red. A blindfolded person picks a blue marble $\frac{1}{4}$ of the time, a green marble $\frac{3}{20}$ of the time and a yellow marble $\frac{1}{5}$ of the time.

a.   What is the probability of picking a marble that is either yellow, green, red or blue? _____

b.   What is the probability that the person will pick a red marble? _____

---

a.   The probability of picking a marble that is either yellow, green, red or blue is $\frac{20}{20}$ or 1. There were only these four colors of marbles in the box.

b.

Probability of Green		Probability of Yellow		Probability of Blue		Probability of Red		Total Probability
$\frac{3}{20}$	+	$\frac{4}{20}$	+	$\frac{5}{20}$	+	$\frac{?}{20}$	=	$\frac{20}{20}$

$$\frac{?}{20} = \frac{20}{20} - \frac{12}{20} = \frac{8}{20} = \frac{2}{5} \text{ probability of picking red}$$

54.   If the probability of having type O blood is $\frac{1}{2}$ and the probability of having type A blood is $\frac{1}{4}$, would you add or multiply the separate probabilities to find the probability of a person having either type O or type A blood? _____

Add

55.   If the probability of having type O blood is $\frac{1}{2}$ and the probability of having type A blood is $\frac{1}{4}$,

a.   What is the probability of a person having either type O or type A blood? _____

b.   What is the probability of having either AB or B blood type? _____

a. Probability of Type O Blood		Probability of Type A Blood		Probability of Either O or A
$\dfrac{1}{2}$	$+$	$\dfrac{1}{4}$	$=$	$\dfrac{3}{4}$

b. Probability of Either A, B, AB or O Blood		Probability of Either O or A Blood		Probability of Either AB or B Blood
1	$-$	$\dfrac{3}{4}$	$=$	$\dfrac{1}{4}$

56. In a particular woods there are eight dead trees—five beech and three maple. Three pairs of owls nest in the woods. Each pair nests in a dead tree and no tree contains more than one nest. Assuming the choice of a nesting site is random,

a. What is the probability of the first pair nesting in a maple? _____

b. In a beech? _____

c. Either a maple or a beech? _____

If the first pair nested in a maple, what is the probability of the second pair nesting in a:

d. maple? _____

e. beech? _____

If the first and second pairs both nested in maples, what is the probability of the third pair nesting in a:

f. maple? _____

g. beech? _____

What is the probability of all three owl pairs simultaneously nesting in maples? _____

a. three chances to nest in a maple out of eight dead trees = $\frac{3}{8}$

b. five chances to nest in a beech out of eight dead trees = $\frac{5}{8}$

c. $\frac{3}{8} + \frac{5}{8} = \frac{8}{8}$ or 1

d. two chances to nest in a maple out of seven dead trees = $\frac{2}{7}$
(One pair has nested in a maple, leaving only seven trees to nest in, only two of which are maples.)

e. $\frac{5}{7}$

f. $\frac{1}{6}$

g. $\frac{5}{6}$

Probability of First Pair in a Maple		Probability of Second Pair in a Maple		Probability of Third Pair in a Maple		Probability of All Three Pairs in Maples
$\frac{3}{8}$	X	$\frac{2}{7}$	X	$\frac{1}{6}$	=	$\frac{6}{336}$ or $\frac{1}{56}$

57. The probability of either one event or the other occurring is equal to the (product/sum) _____ of the individual probabilities.

sum

58. You have now learned two basic principles or generalizations which are useful in determining probabilities:

a. The probability of two or more independent events occurring simultaneously is equal to the (sum/product) _____ of their separate probabilities. (See frame 47.)

b. The probability of either one event or the other occurring is equal to the (product/sum) _____ of their individual probabilities. (See frame 57.)

36

a. **product**   b. **sum**

59. These two principles may be combined in determining probabilities, as illustrated in the following problem:

The probability of rolling two dice and: _____
a. getting either a two or a three on the first die is _____ .
b. getting a six on the second die is _____ .
c. getting a two or a three on the first die and a six on the second die is _____ .

a. The probability of getting a two is $\frac{1}{6}$. _____
The probability of getting a three is $\frac{1}{6}$.
The probability of getting either a two or a three is $\frac{1}{6} + \frac{1}{6}$ or $\frac{2}{6}$ or $\frac{1}{3}$.
b. The probability of getting a six on the second die is $\frac{1}{6}$.

c.

Probability of Either a Two or a Three on First Die		Probability of Getting a Six on Second Die		Probability for Both	
$\frac{2}{6}$	X	$\frac{1}{6}$	=	$\frac{2}{36}$ or $\frac{1}{18}$	

60. In a family consisting of two children, what is the probability of having a boy for the first child and either a boy or a girl for the second child? _____

The probability of having a boy for the first child is $\frac{1}{2}$.
The probability of having either a boy or a girl for the second child is $\frac{1}{2} + \frac{1}{2}$ or 1.
Therefore, the probability of having a boy for the first child and either a boy or a girl for the second child is $\frac{1}{2}$ X 1 or $\frac{1}{2}$.

Progress Quiz: Basic Probability Principles

When you have completed this quiz, check your answers against those provided in Appendix B at the end of this book.

1. Three pennies are simultaneously flipped into the air. How many different possible combinations or orders are there for the three pennies? _____

2. There are 20 commonly occurring amino acids in living organisms. If we know that ten of these 20 amino acids are *not* found in a particular dipeptide, how many different dipeptides are possible? _____

3. The probability of an albino being born to parents, both of whom are heterozygous for the albino gene, is $\frac{1}{4}$. What is the probability of their having an albino girl? _____

4. A couple has two boys. What is the probability of both of their *next* two children being boys? _____

5. What is the probability of rolling a die and getting either a two or a four? _____

6. A number of marbles are put into a box. There are only four colors of marbles. The probability of a blindfolded person's picking a blue marble is $\frac{1}{4}$, a green marble is $\frac{3}{20}$, a yellow marble is $\frac{1}{5}$ and a red marble is $\frac{2}{5}$. What is the probability of picking either a yellow or a red marble? _____

7. a. The probability of either one event or the other occurring at a particular time is equal to the probability of the first event occurring (times/plus)_____the probability of the second event occurring.

b. The probability of two independent events occurring simultaneously is equal to the probability of the first event occurring (times/plus) _____ the probability of the second event occurring.

8. In a family of two children,

a. What is the probability that both will be girls (GG)? _____

b. Both boys (BB)? _____

c.   What is the probability that the first child will be a girl and the second a boy (GB)? _____

d.   What is the probability that the first child will be a boy and the second a girl (BG)? _____

e.   What is the probability of having one boy and one girl in any order? _____

f.   What is the probability that, in a family of two children, there will be either two girls (GG), or two boys (BB), or a girl and a boy (GB) or a boy and a girl (BG)? _____

9.   Suppose that in a DNA molecule, the probability of getting any of the four nitrogen-containing bases at a particular position is $\frac{1}{4}$. What is the probability of getting either the sequence guanine-adenine-cytosine (GAC), or the sequence guanine-guanine-thymine (GGT)? _____

10. Twenty marbles are put into a box. There are four different colors of marbles: five yellow, five green, five blue and five red. On the first trial, a blindfolded person withdraws a green marble and does *not* return it to the box.

a.   What is the probability that, on his second trial, he will pick a green marble? _____

b.   What is the probability that, on his second trial, he will pick a blue marble? _____

c.   What is the probability that, on his second trial, he will pick either a blue, a yellow or a red marble? _____

d.   If, on his second trial, he picked a green marble, and did not return it to the box, what is the probability of his picking a green marble on his third trial? _____

e.   What is the probability of his picking three green marbles?

_____

II
BINOMIAL
EXPANSION

Performance Objectives

As a result of conscientious study of this chapter, you will be able
to:

- expand the binomial $(a + b)^N$;

- explain the significance of the coefficient and exponents in
  each term of the expanded binomial;

- use a shortcut method for calculating the coefficients of the
  terms in the expanded binomial;

- use the expanded binomial in calculating probabilities in
  problems of biological significance, such as the example
  problem in Section 1 of this chapter.

Section 1: *Expanding the Binomial*

Examine the following example problem. This should provide you with guidelines for the work you will be doing in this chapter.

What is the probability that in a family of three children there will be two girls and one boy? The following steps must be considered when answering this question.

Step 1. The three possible orders of birth for two girls and one boy in a family of three children are:

$$\text{Boy—Girl—Girl} \quad \text{(BGG)}$$
$$\text{Girl—Boy—Girl} \quad \text{(GBG)}$$
$$\text{Girl—Girl—Boy} \quad \text{(GGB)}$$

First Child Probability of B		Second Child Probability of G		Third Child Probability of G		Probability of a Family of Three Children Consisting of BGG in That Order
$\frac{1}{2}$	X	$\frac{1}{2}$	X	$\frac{1}{2}$	=	$\frac{1}{8}$
Probability of G		Probability of B		Probability of G		Consisting of GBG in That Order
$\frac{1}{2}$	X	$\frac{1}{2}$	X	$\frac{1}{2}$	=	$\frac{1}{8}$
Probability of G		Probability of G		Probability of B		Consisting of GGB in That Order
$\frac{1}{2}$	X	$\frac{1}{2}$	X	$\frac{1}{2}$	=	$\frac{1}{8}$

Step 2. Any of these three orders (BGG, BGB *or* GGB) is possible for a family of three children consisting of two girls and one boy. Therefore, we *add* the separate probabilities for the various combinations to obtain the probability of a family of three children consisting of two girls and one boy in any order.

43

Probability of BGG	Probability of GBG	Probability of GGB	Probability of Two G and One B in Any Order
$\frac{1}{8}$ +	$\frac{1}{8}$ +	$\frac{1}{8}$ =	$\frac{3}{8}$

Note, the probability for two boys and one girl (BBG, BGB, GBB) is the same—$\frac{3}{8}$. However, the probability of three girls (GGG) is $\frac{1}{8}$ because there is only *one order* in which there could be three girls:

Probability of a Girl	Probability of a Girl	Probability of a Girl	Probability of GGG
$\frac{1}{2}$ X	$\frac{1}{2}$ X	$\frac{1}{2}$ =	$\frac{1}{8}$

Likewise, the probability of three boys (BBB) is $\frac{1}{8}$.

61. Recall that there are *four* different nitrogen-containing bases that may occur in the nucleotides that make up the DNA molecule. Assume that all four bases are equally available.

a. What is the probability that any *one* of the four bases will occur at a particular position? _____

b. In a three-nucleotide sequence, what are the possible combinations of two guanine molecules (G) and one adenine molecule (A)? _____

c. What is the probability of two guanine molecules and one adenine molecule occurring in the sequence GGA? _____

d. What is the probability of the sequence GAG? _____

e. What is the probability of the sequence AGG? _____

f. What is the probability that in a three-nucleotide sequence the bases will be two G and one A in any order? _____

a. The probability of one of the four possible bases occurring at a given position in the nucleotide sequence is $\frac{1}{4}$.

b. The possible combinations are GGA, GAG and AGG.

c. The probability of the sequence GGA is $\frac{1}{4} \times \frac{1}{4} \times \frac{1}{4}$ or $\frac{1}{64}$.

d. The probability of the sequence GAG is $\frac{1}{4} \times \frac{1}{4} \times \frac{1}{4}$ or $\frac{1}{64}$.

e. The probability of the sequence AGG is $\frac{1}{4} \times \frac{1}{4} \times \frac{1}{4}$ or $\frac{1}{64}$.

f. The probability of having two guanine and one adenine molecules in a three-base sequence is $\frac{1}{64} + \frac{1}{64} + \frac{1}{64}$ or $\frac{3}{64}$.

62. In a family of four children, three are girls and one is a boy.

a. What are the possible orders of birth of girls and boys for this family? _____

b. What is the probability of the birth order BGGG? _____

c. Of the birth order GBGG? _____

d. Of the birth order GGBG? _____

e. Of the birth order GGGB? _____

f. What is the probability that, in a family of four children, three will be girls and one will be a boy? _____

a. The four possible birth orders are BGGG, GBGG, GGBG and GGGB.

b. The probability of BGGG is $\frac{1}{2} \times \frac{1}{2} \times \frac{1}{2} \times \frac{1}{2}$ or $\frac{1}{16}$.

c. The probability of GBGG is $\frac{1}{2} \times \frac{1}{2} \times \frac{1}{2} \times \frac{1}{2}$ or $\frac{1}{16}$.

d. The probability of GGBG is $\frac{1}{2} \times \frac{1}{2} \times \frac{1}{2} \times \frac{1}{2}$ or $\frac{1}{16}$.

e. The probability of GGGB is $\frac{1}{2} \times \frac{1}{2} \times \frac{1}{2} \times \frac{1}{2}$ or $\frac{1}{16}$.

f.

Probability of BGGG		Probability of GBGG		Probability of GGBG		Probability of GGGB		Probability of Three G Plus One B in Any Order
$\frac{1}{16}$	$+$	$\frac{1}{16}$	$+$	$\frac{1}{16}$	$+$	$\frac{1}{16}$	$=$	$\frac{4}{16}$ or $\frac{1}{4}$

63. In a family of four children,

a. What is the probability that all four will be boys? _____
b. All four will be girls? _____

---

a.

Probability of a Boy		Probability of a Boy		Probability of a Boy		Probability of a Boy		Probability of Four Boys
$\frac{1}{2}$	$\times$	$\frac{1}{2}$	$\times$	$\frac{1}{2}$	$\times$	$\frac{1}{2}$	$=$	$\frac{1}{16}$

b. Likewise, the probability of four girls is $\frac{1}{16}$.

64. A card is drawn from a 52-card deck.

a. What is the probability that the card will be a heart? _____
b. What is the probability that it will be a spade? _____

---

a. The probability of drawing a heart is $\frac{13}{52}$ or $\frac{1}{4}$.
b. The probability of drawing a spade is $\frac{13}{52}$ or $\frac{1}{4}$.

65. Four cards are drawn, each from a *different* deck of 52 cards.

a. Assuming that three hearts (H) and one spade (S) are drawn,

what are the different orders in which they could be drawn?
_____

b.   What is the probability that three of the cards will be hearts and one of them will be a spade in any order? _____

---

a.   The three hearts and one spade can be drawn in these four different orders: HHHS, HHSH, HSHH or SHHH.

b.   The probability of HHHS is $\frac{13}{52} \times \frac{13}{52} \times \frac{13}{52} \times \frac{13}{52}$, which is $\frac{1}{256}$, or $\frac{1}{4} \times \frac{1}{4} \times \frac{1}{4} \times \frac{1}{4}$, which is also $\frac{1}{256}$.

The probability of HHSH is $\frac{1}{4} \times \frac{1}{4} \times \frac{1}{4} \times \frac{1}{4}$ or $\frac{1}{256}$.

The probability of HSHH is $\frac{1}{4} \times \frac{1}{4} \times \frac{1}{4} \times \frac{1}{4}$ or $\frac{1}{256}$.

The probability of SHHH is $\frac{1}{4} \times \frac{1}{4} \times \frac{1}{4} \times \frac{1}{4}$ or $\frac{1}{256}$.

The probability of drawing three hearts and one spade in any order is $\frac{1}{256} + \frac{1}{256} + \frac{1}{256} + \frac{4}{256}$ or $\frac{1}{64}$.

66.   In a family of five children,

a.   How many different orders of birth are possible for three boys and two girls? _____
b.   What are the different orders? _____

---

c.   What is the probability for any *one* particular order of birth of the ten possible orders? _____
d.   In a family of five children, what is the probability of having three boys and two girls in any order? _____

a. There are ten possible orders of birth for three boys and two girls in a family of five children.

b. The orders are BBBGG, BBGGB, BGGBB, GGBBB, GBBBG, BBGBG, BGBGB, BGBBG, GBBBG and GBGBB.

c. The probability for any *one* of the ten possible orders is $\frac{1}{32}$, as shown below:

probability of BBBGG $= \frac{1}{2} \times \frac{1}{2} \times \frac{1}{2} \times \frac{1}{2} \times \frac{1}{2} = \frac{1}{32}$

probability of BBGGB $= \frac{1}{2} \times \frac{1}{2} \times \frac{1}{2} \times \frac{1}{2} \times \frac{1}{2} = \frac{1}{32}$

probability of BGGBB $= \frac{1}{2} \times \frac{1}{2} \times \frac{1}{2} \times \frac{1}{2} \times \frac{1}{2} = \frac{1}{32}$

probability of GGBBB $= \frac{1}{2} \times \frac{1}{2} \times \frac{1}{2} \times \frac{1}{2} \times \frac{1}{2} = \frac{1}{32}$

probability of GBBBG $= \frac{1}{2} \times \frac{1}{2} \times \frac{1}{2} \times \frac{1}{2} \times \frac{1}{2} = \frac{1}{32}$

probability of BBGBG $= \frac{1}{2} \times \frac{1}{2} \times \frac{1}{2} \times \frac{1}{2} \times \frac{1}{2} = \frac{1}{32}$

probability of BGBGB $= \frac{1}{2} \times \frac{1}{2} \times \frac{1}{2} \times \frac{1}{2} \times \frac{1}{2} = \frac{1}{32}$

probability of BGBBG $= \frac{1}{2} \times \frac{1}{2} \times \frac{1}{2} \times \frac{1}{2} \times \frac{1}{2} = \frac{1}{32}$

probability of GBBBG $= \frac{1}{2} \times \frac{1}{2} \times \frac{1}{2} \times \frac{1}{2} \times \frac{1}{2} = \frac{1}{32}$

probability of GBGBB $= \frac{1}{2} \times \frac{1}{2} \times \frac{1}{2} \times \frac{1}{2} \times \frac{1}{2} = \frac{1}{32}$

d. The probability of having three boys and two girls in any order is $\frac{1}{32} + \frac{1}{32} + \frac{1}{32} + \frac{1}{32} + \frac{1}{32} + \frac{1}{32} + \frac{1}{32} + \frac{1}{32} + \frac{1}{32} + \frac{1}{32}$, which is $\frac{10}{32}$ or $\frac{5}{16}$.

67. In a family of five children, what is the probability of having two *boys* and three *girls* in any order? _____

The probability of having three girls and two boys in a family of five children is $\frac{10}{32}$ or $\frac{5}{16}$. (For explanation, see frame 66.)

68. In a family of five children,

a. How many different orders of birth are there for four boys and one girl? _____
b. What are these different orders? _____

c. What is the probability for any *one* particular order of birth of the five possible orders? _____
d. In a family of five children, what is the probability of having four boys and one girl in any order? _____

---

a. There are five possible orders of birth for four boys and one girl in a family consisting of five children.
b. The different orders of birth are BBBBG, BBBGB, BBGBB, BGBBB and GBBBB.
c. The probability of any one of the five different orders is $\frac{1}{32}$, as shown below:

probability of BBBBG $= \frac{1}{2} \times \frac{1}{2} \times \frac{1}{2} \times \frac{1}{2} \times \frac{1}{2} = \frac{1}{32}$

probability of BBBGB $= \frac{1}{2} \times \frac{1}{2} \times \frac{1}{2} \times \frac{1}{2} \times \frac{1}{2} = \frac{1}{32}$

probability of BBGBB $= \frac{1}{2} \times \frac{1}{2} \times \frac{1}{2} \times \frac{1}{2} \times \frac{1}{2} = \frac{1}{32}$

probability of BGBBB $= \frac{1}{2} \times \frac{1}{2} \times \frac{1}{2} \times \frac{1}{2} \times \frac{1}{2} = \frac{1}{32}$

probability of GBBBB $= \frac{1}{2} \times \frac{1}{2} \times \frac{1}{2} \times \frac{1}{2} \times \frac{1}{2} = \frac{1}{32}$

d. The probability of having four boys and one girl in any order is $\frac{1}{32} + \frac{1}{32} + \frac{1}{32} + \frac{1}{32} + \frac{1}{32}$, or $\frac{5}{32}$.

69. In a family of five children, what is the probability of having *four girls* and *one boy* in any order? _____

The probability of having four girls and one boy in a family of five children is $\frac{5}{32}$. (For explanation, see frame 68.)

70. In a family of five children,

a. What is the probability that all five children will be boys?
_____

b. All five children will be girls? _____

---

a. Since there is *only one* order of five boys (BBBBB), the probability that all five children will be boys is $\frac{1}{2} \times \frac{1}{2} \times \frac{1}{2} \times \frac{1}{2} \times \frac{1}{2}$ or $\frac{1}{32}$.

b. Likewise, the probability that all five children will be girls is $\frac{1}{32}$.

71. The answers for frames 66-70 may be worked out much more easily in another way known as *expansion of the binomial*. This method will be investigated next.

A binomial has two terms: *a*, which represents the probability of one event, and *b*, which represents the probability of the alternative event. To expand the binomial, raise it to a specific *power*, that power being the number of events involved in the particular problem. For example, you can have $(a + b)^2$, $(a + b)^3$, $(a + b)^4$, and so on. In other words, the binomial can be shown as $(a + b)^N$, where N = _____ .

---

the total number of events being considered

72. The binomial expansion principle can be used in working probability problems *only* when the sum of the probabilities of the events is equal to one. Therefore, (a + b) must always be equal to _____ .

---

one

73. To expand the binomial $(a + b)^2$, multiply (a + b) by (a + b). What is the product obtained when you expand the binomial $(a + b)^2$? _____

$a^2 + 2ab + b^2$
If your answer is *correct*, go to frame 75.
If your answer is *incorrect*, go to frame 74.

74. The product of $(a + b)^2$ may be obtained as follows:

$$(a + b)^2 = (a + b) \times (a + b)$$

This may be written with one term above the other for ease in multiplying.

$$\begin{array}{r} (a + b) \\ \times \ \underline{(a + b)} \end{array}$$

Multiply each term of one binomial by each term of the other binomial. Starting with the b of the lower binomial, $b \times b = b^2$ and $b \times a = ab$. In the problem, this appears as:

$$\begin{array}{r} (a + b) \\ \times \ (a + b) \\ \hline ab + b^2 \end{array}$$

Now, multiplying by the a of the lower binomial, $a \times a = a^2$ and $a \times b = ab$. The problem now appears as:

$$\begin{array}{r} (a + b) \\ \times \ (a + b) \\ \hline ab + b^2 \\ a^2 + ab \end{array}$$

Add to get the final product, just as in ordinary multiplication. Therefore, the expansion of $(a + b)^2$ is: (Write the answer in the box below.)

$$\begin{array}{r} (a + b) \\ \times \ (a + b) \\ \hline ab + b^2 \\ a^2 + ab \end{array}$$

$$\boxed{}$$

$a^2 + 2ab + b^2$
If your answer is incorrect, restudy frame 74.

75. Expand the binomial $(a + b)^3$. The product obtained is

_____ .

$a^3 + 3a^2b + 3ab^2 + b^3$

If your answer is *correct*, go to frame 77.

If your answer is *incorrect*, go to frame 76.

76. The product of $(a + b)^3$ may be obtained as follows:

$$(a + b)^3 = (a + b) \times (a + b) \times (a + b)$$

$$
\begin{array}{r}
(a + b) \\
\times \ (a + b) \\
\hline
ab + b^2 \\
a^2 + ab \\
\hline
a^2 + 2ab + b^2 \\
\times \ (a + b) \\
\hline
a^2b + 2ab^2 + b^3 \\
a^3 + 2a^2b + \ ab^2 \\
\hline
\end{array}
$$

$$\boxed{}$$

However, since you already have expanded $(a + b)^2$, it might be easier to expand $(a + b)^3$ in the following way:

$$(a + b)^3 = (a + b)^2 \times (a + b)$$
$$(a + b)^2 = a^2 + 2ab + b^2$$

Therefore, $(a + b)^3 = (a + b)^2 \times (a + b)$

$$
\begin{array}{r}
a^2 + 2ab + b^2 \\
\times \quad a + b \\
\hline
a^2b + 2ab^2 + b^3 \\
a^3 + 2a^2b + \ ab^2 \\
\hline
\end{array}
$$

$$\boxed{}$$

The product obtained in either manner is $a^3 + 3a^2b + 3ab^2 + b^3$.

77. Now, expand the binomial $(a + b)^4$. Remember, $(a + b)^4 =$ $(a + b) \times (a + b) \times (a + b) \times (a + b)$ *or* $(a + b)^3 \times (a + b)$. The product obtained when you expand the binomial $(a + b)^4$ is

_____ .

$(a + b)^4 = a^4 + 4a^3b + 6a^2b^2 + 4ab^3 + b^4$
If your answer is *correct*, go to frame 79.
If your answer is *incorrect*, go to frame 78.

78. a.   The product of $(a + b)^4 =$

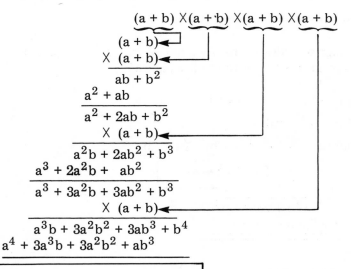

b.   Or, you can solve the problem this way: (Fill in the seven missing lines.)

$(a + b)^4 = (a + b)^2 \times (a + b)^2$

$(a + b)^2 =$

Therefore, $(a + b)^4 = (a + b)^2 \times (a + b)^2$

---

a. $(a + b)^4 = a^4 + 4a^3b + 6a^2b^2 + 4ab^3 + b^4$

b. $(a + b)^2 = a^2 + 2ab + b^2$

Therefore, $(a + b)^4 =$

$$
\begin{array}{r}
a^2 + 2ab + b^2 \\
\times\ a^2 + 2ab + b^2 \\
\hline
a^2b^2 + 2ab^3 + b^4 \\
2a^3b + 4a^2b^2 + 2ab^3 \\
a^4 + 2a^3b + a^2b^2 \\
\hline
a^4 + 4a^3b + 6a^2b^2 + 4ab^3 + b^4
\end{array}
$$

79. Expand the binomial $(a + b)^5$. The product of $(a + b)^5$ is

_____ .

$a^5 + 5a^4b + 10a^3b^2 + 10a^2b^3 + 5ab^4 + b^5$
If your answer is *correct*, go to frame 81.
If your answer is *incorrect*, go to frame 80.

80. Expansion of $(a + b)^5$ is: (Fill in the six missing lines.)
$(a + b) \times (a + b) \times (a + b) \times (a + b) \times (a + b) = (a + b)^3 \times (a + b)^2$.

X _____

‎

‎

$(a + b)^5 = (a + b)^3 \times (a + b)^2 =$

$$
\begin{array}{r}
a^3 + 3a^2b + 3ab^2 + b^3 \\
\times \quad a^2 + 2ab + b^2 \\
\hline
a^3b^2 + 3a^2b^3 + 3ab^4 + b^5 \\
2a^4b + 6a^3b^2 + 6a^2b^3 + 2ab^4 \\
a^5 + 3a^4b + 3a^3b^2 + a^2b^3 \\
\hline
a^5 + 5a^4b + 10a^3b^2 + 10a^2b^3 + 5ab^4 + b^5
\end{array}
$$

81. We are now prepared to use this binomial expansion principle in solving probability problems. In the binomial $(a + b)^N$, let a equal the probability of one event occurring and b equal the probability of the alternative event occurring. We will consider a family of three children.

a.   Remember, N = _____ .
b.   In this case, N = _____ .
c.   The probability of having a girl (a) plus the probability of having a boy (b) must equal _____ .

---

a.   the total number of events we are considering
b.   the three children or 3
c.   1

82. Since we are considering three events (in this case, children), we will use the expanded binomial $(a + b)^3$. Remember, a is the probability of having a girl ($\frac{1}{2}$) and b is the probability of having a boy ($\frac{1}{2}$). We know that $(a + b) = (\frac{1}{2} + \frac{1}{2}) = 1$. The expanded binomial $(a + b)^3 = \boxed{a^3} + 3a^2b + 3ab^2 + b^3$.

The first term, a^3, may be interpreted as follows:

> The a stands for the probability of the first event, in this case, the probability of having a girl. The superscript 3 (cube symbol) means that a is multiplied by a and by a again. In this case, the a^3 would give the probability of having three girls in a family of three children.

What is the probability of having three girls in a family of three children? _____

For finding the probability of having three girls in a family of three children you must substitute the probability of having a girl

$(\frac{1}{2})$ for a and since you are concerned with the probability of three girls, the term we use is a^3.

Therefore, $a^3 = (\frac{1}{2})^3 = \frac{1}{8}$ = the probability of having three girls in a family of three children.

83. From the expanded binomial $(a + b)^3 = a^3 + \boxed{3a^2b} + 3ab^2 + b^3$, the second term, $3a^2b$, may be interpreted as follows:

> The coefficient, 3, indicates that there are three possible combinations or orders of events. In this case, there are three different orders of birth for one boy and two girls. The a is the probability of having a girl and b is the probability of having a boy. The superscript 2 of the a in the term $3a^2b$ refers to having two girls and the superscript 1 (understood) of the b refers to having one boy. Note that the sum of the exponents $(2 + 1)$ equals the total number of events (children).

In a family of three children, what is the probability of having two girls and one boy in any order? _____

The term to use is $3a^2b$. Now, substitute the probability of having a girl $(\frac{1}{2})$ for a and the probability of having a boy $(\frac{1}{2})$ for b.

Therefore, $3a^2b = 3 (\frac{1}{2})^2 \times (\frac{1}{2}) = 3 \times \frac{1}{2} \times \frac{1}{2} \times \frac{1}{2} = \frac{3}{8}$ = the probability of having two girls and one boy in a family of three children.

84. From the expanded binomial $(a + b)^3 = a^3 + 3a^2b + \boxed{3ab^2} + b^3$ the third term, $3ab^2$, may be interpreted as follows:

> The coefficient, 3, indicates that there are three possible combinations or orders of events. In this case, there are

three different orders of birth for two boys and one girl. The a is the probability of having a girl and b is the probability of having a boy. The superscript 1 (understood) of the a refers to having one girl and the superscript 2 of the b refers to having two boys.

In a family of three children, what is the probability of having one girl and two boys in any order? _____

The term we are interested in is $3ab^2$. Substituting $\frac{1}{2}$ for a and $\frac{1}{2}$ for b we have $3ab^2 = 3(\frac{1}{2}) \times (\frac{1}{2})^2 = 3 \times \frac{1}{2} \times \frac{1}{2} \times \frac{1}{2} = \frac{3}{8}$ = the probability of having one girl and two boys in a family of three children.

85. The last term of the expanded binomial $(a + b)^3 = a^3 + 3a^2b + 3ab^2 + \boxed{b^3}$ may be interpreted as follows:

The b is the probability of the alternative event, in this case, the probability of having a boy. The superscript $(^3)$ means that b is multiplied by b and by b again. In this case, the b^3 would be the probability of having three boys in a family of three children.

What is the probability of having three boys in a family of three children? _____

The term we are interested in is b^3. Substituting the probability of having a boy $(\frac{1}{2})$ for b, $b^3 = (\frac{1}{2})^3 = \frac{1}{8}$ = the probability of having three boys in a family of three children.

86. From the expansion of the binomial, $(a + b)^5$:

a. Which term represents the probability of having five girls in a family consisting of five children? _____

b. What is the probability of having five girls in a family consisting of five children? _____

---

a. Expansion of the binomial $(a + b)^5$ gives $a^5 + 5a^4b + 10a^3b^2 + 10a^2b^3 + 5ab^4 + b^5$. The term which represents the probability of having five girls in a family of five children is a^5, where *a* represents the probability of having a girl ($\frac{1}{2}$) and the superscript or exponent, 5, means five girls.

b. The probability of having five girls in a family of five children can be found quickly by substituting the probability of a girl ($\frac{1}{2}$) for *a*. Therefore, $a^5 = \frac{1}{2} \times \frac{1}{2} \times \frac{1}{2} \times \frac{1}{2} \times \frac{1}{2} = \frac{1}{32}$.

87. From the expansion of the binomial $(a + b)^5$,

a. Which term represents the probability of having five boys in a family consisting of five children? _____

b. What is the probability of having five boys in a family consisting of five children? _____

c. Which term represents the probability of having four girls and one boy in any order? _____

d. In a family of five children, what is the probability of having four girls and one boy in any order? _____

a.   Expansion of the binomial $(a + b)^5$ gives $a^5 + 5a^4b + 10a^3b^2 + 10a^2b^3 + 5ab^4 + b^5$. The term which represents the probability of having five boys in a family of five children is b^5, where b represents the probability of having a boy $(\frac{1}{2})$ and the exponent, 5, means five boys.

b.   The probability of having five boys in a family consisting of five children $= b^5 = (\frac{1}{2})^5 = \frac{1}{2} \times \frac{1}{2} \times \frac{1}{2} \times \frac{1}{2} \times \frac{1}{2} = \frac{1}{32}$.

c.   The term which represents the probability of having four girls and one boy in any order is $5a^4b$, where a represents the probability of a girl $(\frac{1}{2})$ and the exponent, 4, means four girls. The b represents the probability of a boy $(\frac{1}{2})$ and the exponent, 1 (understood), means one boy. The coefficient, 5, means there are five different orders or combinations of four girls and one boy for a family of five children. These five orders are BGGGG, GBGGG, GGBGG, GGGBG, GGGGB.

d.   In a family of five children, the probability of having four girls and one boy in any order is: $5a^4b = 5(\frac{1}{2})^4 \times (\frac{1}{2}) = 5 \times \frac{1}{2} \times \frac{1}{2} \times \frac{1}{2} \times \frac{1}{2} \times \frac{1}{2} = \frac{5}{32}$.

88.   In a family consisting of five children, what is the probability of having one girl and four boys in any order? _____

The term of the expanded binomial $(a + b)^5$ that we are interested in is $5ab^4$, which represents the probability of having one girl and four boys in a family of five children. Substituting, $5ab^4 = 5(\frac{1}{2}) \times (\frac{1}{2})^4 = 5 \times \frac{1}{2} \times \frac{1}{2} \times \frac{1}{2} \times \frac{1}{2} \times \frac{1}{2} = \frac{5}{32}$.

89.   In a family consisting of five children,

a.   What is the probability of having three girls and two boys?

_____

b. What is the probability of having two girls and three boys?

———

a. The term of the expanded binomial $(a + b)^5$ to use is $10a^3b^2$, where the coefficient, 10, represents the ten different orders (GGGBB, GGBBG, and so on) in which there can be three girls and two boys in a family of five children. Substituting, you get $10a^3b^2 = 10 \left(\frac{1}{2}\right)^3 \times \left(\frac{1}{2}\right)^2 = 10 \times \frac{1}{2} \times \frac{1}{2} \times \frac{1}{2} \times \frac{1}{2} \times \frac{1}{2} = \frac{10}{32} = \frac{5}{16} =$ the probability of having three girls and two boys in a family of five children.

b. The term which represents the probability of having two girls and three boys in a family of five children is $10a^2b^3$. Substituting,
$10a^2b^3 = 10 \left(\frac{1}{2}\right)^2 \times \left(\frac{1}{2}\right)^3 = 10 \times \frac{1}{2} \times \frac{1}{2} \times \frac{1}{2} \times \frac{1}{2} \times \frac{1}{2} = \frac{10}{32} = \frac{5}{16}.$

90. Two individuals, both heterozygous for the gene D, are mated. The probability (a) of the offspring showing the dominant gene, D, is $\frac{3}{4}$. The probability (b) of the offspring showing the recessive gene, d, is $\frac{1}{4}$. Using the binomial expansion method, calculate the probability that, in a family of five children, three of them will express the D gene, and two of them, the d gene.

Since we are concerned with five events (three offspring express-ing D plus two offspring expressing d), we expand the binomial $(a + b)^5$ to give $a^5 + 5a^4b + 10a^3b^2 + 10a^2b^3 + 5ab^4 + b^5$. The term to use is $10a^3b^2$ because there are 10 different orders in which there could be three children showing the dominant gene D and two children showing the recessive gene d. Substituting $\frac{3}{4}$ for a (the probability of expressing D) and $\frac{1}{4}$ for b (the proba-bility of expressing d): $10a^3b^2 = 10 \times (\frac{3}{4})^3 \times (\frac{1}{4})^2 = 10 \times \frac{3}{4} \times \frac{3}{4} \times \frac{3}{4} \times \frac{1}{4} \times \frac{1}{4} = \frac{270}{1,024} = \frac{135}{512}$ or about $\frac{1}{3.79}$.

91. Fortunately, there are shortcuts for finding the exponents and coefficients in expanding the binomial.

The shortcut for the determination of exponents may already be obvious to you.

a. Expand the binomial $(a + b)^5$.
   Note that as the exponent of an a decreases, the exponent of b increases. The exponent of a always begins with the number which equals the N value, and decreases to 1 (which is understood), and finally to 0. It should be mentioned that $a^0 = 1$. Likewise, $b^0 = 1$. However, note that in each term the sum of the exponents of a and b equals the N value, in this case, 5.

b. Therefore, in the binomial $(a + b)^5$, a and its exponents progress as follows: a^5, _____, _____, _____, _____, a^0 or 1.

c. In reverse order, b and its exponents progress as follows: b^0 or 1, _____, _____, _____, _____.

a. $a^5 + 5a^4b + 10a^3b^2 + 10a^2b^3 + 5ab^4 + b^5$
b. a^4, a^3, a^2, a^1 or a
c. b^1 or b, b^2, b^3, b^4, b^5

92. Expand the binomial $(a + b)^6$, showing a and b with their exponents *only*. (Do not be concerned at this time about the coefficients.)

$a^6 + a^5b + a^4b^2 + a^3b^3 + a^2b^4 + ab^5 + b^6$

93. Now you will learn a shortcut for determining the coefficients. Consider the expansion of $(a + b)^5$ again. The coefficient of the first term (in this case a^5) is always 1. Usually, the 1 is not written but is understood.

a. The coefficient of the second term may be determined by multiplying the coefficient of the first term (which is always _____) by the exponent of a of the first term, which in this case is _____ . This gives _____ .
b. Then, divide this value by the number of the preceding term in the expansion, which in this case is 1. Therefore, the coefficient of the second term is _____ .

a. 1; 5; 5
b. 5

94. The succeeding coefficients are determined by employing the same method you have just used. *That is, the coefficient for any particular term is equal to the product of the coefficient and the exponent of a of the preceding term divided by the number of the preceding term in the expanded binomial.* To illustrate, from the expanded binomial $(a + b)^5$, the coefficient of the third term may be obtained as follows:

Coefficient of Preceding Term		Exponent of a of Preceding Term		Number of Preceding Term		Desired Coefficient
5	X	4	÷	2	=	10

That is, the coefficient of the third term is _____ .

10

95. Now, complete the binomial expansion of $(a + b)^5$, calculating the coefficients of the various terms by the method just explained.

Number of Desired Coefficient	Coefficient of Preceding Term		Exponent of a of Preceding Term		Number of Preceding Term		Desired Coefficient
fourth	_____	X	_____	÷	_____	=	_____
fifth	_____	X	_____	÷	_____	=	_____
sixth	_____	X	_____	÷	_____	=	_____

---

coefficient of the fourth term = 10 X 3 ÷ 3 = 10
coefficient of the fifth term = 10 X 2 ÷ 4 = 5
coefficient of the sixth term = 5 X 1 ÷ 5 = 1

96. Expand the binomial $(a + b)^4$ using the shortcuts for determining the exponents and coefficients.

The exponents of the expanded binomial $(a + b)^4$ are:
$a^4 + a^3b + a^2b^2 + ab^3 + b^4$
The first coefficient is 1.
Other coefficients are:

Number of Desired Coefficient	Coefficient of Preceding Term		Exponent of a of Preceding Term		Number of Preceding Term		Desired Coefficient
second	1	X	4	÷	1	=	4
third	4	X	3	÷	2	=	6
fourth	6	X	2	÷	3	=	4
fifth	4	X	1	÷	4	=	1

Therefore, the expanded binomial $(a + b)^4$ is
$a^4 + 4a^3b + 6a^2b^2 + 4ab^3 + b^4$.

97. Expand the binomial $(a + b)^6$ using the shortcuts for determining the exponents and coefficients.

The exponents of the expanded binomial $(a + b)^6$ are
$a^6 + a^5b + a^4b^2 + a^3b^3 + a^2b^4 + ab^5 + b^6$.
The coefficient of the first term is 1.

Number of Desired Coefficient	Coefficient of Preceding Term		Exponent of a of Preceding Term		Number of Preceding Term		Desired Coefficient
second	1	X	6	÷	1	=	6
third	6	X	5	÷	2	=	15
fourth	15	X	4	÷	3	=	20
fifth	20	X	3	÷	4	=	15
sixth	15	X	2	÷	5	=	6
seventh	6	X	1	÷	6	=	1

Therefore, the expanded binomial $(a + b)^6$ is
$a^6 + 6a^5b + 15a^4b^2 + 20a^3b^3 + 15a^2b^4 + 6ab^5 + b^6$.

98. a.   To summarize, a quick method of determining the specific total probability for two alternative events which occur a number of times in a number of ways or orders is to use

_____ .

b.   However, before you can use this method you must first determine the probability of the one event and the probability of

_____ .

c.   You must also remember that the probability of the first event (times/plus) _____ the probability of the alternative event must be _____ .

a.   the binomial expansion principle
b.   the alternative event
c.   plus; 1

Progress Quiz II. A: Expanding the Binomial

When you have completed this quiz, check your answers against those provided in appendix B at the end of this book.

1.   A couple has three children. You are asked to calculate various probabilities concerning the different orders of birth for these three children. If you use the binomial expansion principle, you would expand the binomial (a + b) to the _____ power.

2.   A couple has three children. Which term of the appropriate binomial expansion would represent the probability of their having one girl and two boys in any order? _____

3.   a. $10a^3b^2$ represents a term in the expanded binomial (a + b) to what power?_____ The probability of one event occurring is represented by _____ . The probability of the alternative event occurring is represented by_____ .
b.   The number of times the event having probability *a* occurs is_____ (the exponent of *a*).
c.   The exponent of _____ (^{2}) equals _____
_____ .
d.   The coefficient, 10, equals the_____ of possible ways in which you could have a^3 and b^2.

4.   Expand the binomial $(a + b)^7$, showing *a* and *b* with their *exponents* only. Use the shortcut method.

5.   Complete the expansion of the binomial $(a + b)^7$, using the shortcut method for determining the coefficients.

---

6.   In a family consisting of seven children,

a.   What is the probability that there will be four girls and three boys in any order? _____

b.   What is the probability that all seven will be boys? _____

Section 2: The Binomial Expansion Principle, Calculating Probabilities, and Solving Genetics Problems

99. In man, A represents the gene for normal skin pigmentation and a represents its allele, which causes albinism when homozygous. If two individuals, both heterozygous (Aa) for this allele have children, the following results are expected:

$\frac{1}{4}$ of offspring AA (normal)

$\frac{1}{2}$ of offspring Aa (normal)

$\frac{1}{4}$ of offspring aa (albino)

In the binomial (a + b), a is the probability of a normal child ($\frac{3}{4}$) and b is the probability of a child with albinism ($\frac{1}{4}$). If this heterozygous couple has three children, what is the probability that two of their three children will be albinos? _____

The expanded binomial $(a + b)^3 = a^3 + 3a^2b + 3ab^2 + b^3$. Since a of the binomial is the probability of a normal child ($\frac{1}{4} + \frac{1}{2}$ or $\frac{3}{4}$) and b is the probability of a child with albinism ($\frac{1}{4}$), the term $3ab^2$ can be used. The coefficient means that there are three ways we can get one normal child and two with albinism. Substituting, $3ab^2 = 3 \times (\frac{3}{4}) \times (\frac{1}{4})^2 = 3 \times \frac{3}{4} \times \frac{1}{4} \times \frac{1}{4} = \frac{9}{64}$.

In other words, the probability of two of the three children having albinism, if both of their parents are heterozygous for the trait, is about nine chances out of 64.

100. The gene for deafness in dogs is recessive, *d*, to the gene for normal hearing, *D*. If two dogs, each heterozygous for this trait, are mated, these are the results expected for the offspring:

$\frac{1}{4}$ *DD* (homozygous for normal hearing)

$\frac{1}{2}$ *Dd* (heterozygous for normal hearing)

$\frac{1}{4}$ *dd* (homozygous and deaf)

From such a cross of two heterozygotes, what is the probability of getting three dogs having normal hearing and two dogs that are deaf from a litter of five? _____

Expand the binomial $(a + b)^5$ to get
$a^5 + 5a^4b + 10a^3b^2 + 10a^2b^3 + 5ab^4 + b^5$.
Since you want the probability of three dogs having normal hearing and two dogs that are deaf, the term to use is $10a^3b^2$, meaning there are ten different orders of getting three dogs having normal hearing and two dogs that are deaf. The probability (*a*) of getting a dog with normal hearing is $\frac{1}{4} + \frac{1}{2}$ or $\frac{3}{4}$ and the probability (*b*) of getting a deaf dog is $\frac{1}{4}$.
Therefore,
$10a^3b^2 = 10 \times (\frac{3}{4})^3 \times (\frac{1}{4})^2 = 10 \times \frac{3}{4} \times \frac{3}{4} \times \frac{3}{4} \times \frac{1}{4} \times \frac{1}{4} = \frac{270}{1,024} = \frac{135}{512}$.

101. In shorthorn cattle, *R* represents the gene for red coat color and *r* represents the gene for white coat color. If an individual is heterozygous, *Rr*, both genes are expressed, resulting in a roan coat color. If a roan male is crossed with a roan female, the expected results are:

$\frac{1}{4}$ of offspring RR—red coat color

$\frac{1}{2}$ of offspring Rr—roan coat color

$\frac{1}{4}$ of offspring rr—white coat color

Five such matings of roan cattle were made, and five offspring were produced. What is the probability that among these five offspring, two will be red and three will be either roan or white (non-red)? _____

The probability of red is a ($\frac{1}{4}$). The probability of a roan or white is b ($\frac{1}{2} + \frac{1}{4}$ or $\frac{3}{4}$). Expand the binomial $(a + b)^5$ and use the term $10a^2b^3$ to substitute. Therefore,

$10 \times (\frac{1}{4})^2 \times (\frac{3}{4})^3 = 10 \times \frac{1}{4} \times \frac{1}{4} \times \frac{3}{4} \times \frac{3}{4} \times \frac{3}{4} = \frac{270}{1,024} = \frac{135}{512}$ or about $\frac{1}{3.79}$.

102. For summer squash, the gene for white fruit, W, is dominant over the gene for colored fruit, w, and the disc-shaped fruit, S, is dominant over the sphere-shaped fruit, s. If two plants, both heterozygous for both genes, are crossed (i.e., $WwSs \times WwSs$), the probability of getting a pure dominant genotype ($WWSS$) is $\frac{1}{16}$ and the probability of getting any other genotype is $\frac{15}{16}$. If a cross like the one described above is made, what is the probability of getting seven consecutive squash with the pure dominant genotype? _____

Expand the binomial $(a + b)^7$ to get
$a^7 + 7a^6b + 21a^5b^2 + 35a^4b^3 + 35a^3b^4 + 21a^2b^5 + 7ab^6 + b^7$.
The probability of obtaining a squash plant with the homozygous dominant genotype is a or $\frac{1}{16}$. The term to use is the first term in the binomial expansion, a^7. Therefore,
$a^7 = (\frac{1}{16})^7 = \frac{1}{16} \times \frac{1}{16} \times \frac{1}{16} \times \frac{1}{16} \times \frac{1}{16} \times \frac{1}{16} \times \frac{1}{16} = \frac{1}{268,435,456} =$ the probability of seven consecutive squash with the pure dominant genotype from the dihybrid cross $WwSs \times WwSs$.

103. In pea plants, W represents the gene for round seeds and w is the allele for wrinkled seeds. Y represents the gene for yellow seeds and y is the allele for green seeds. If a green wrinkled plant $(yyww)$ is crossed with a yellow round plant $(YYWW)$, F_1 hybrids having the genotype $YyWw$ are produced. If a hybrid is self-pollinated, the expected phenotypic ratio in the F_2 generation is:

$\frac{9}{16}$ yellow round
$\frac{3}{16}$ yellow wrinkled
$\frac{3}{16}$ green round
$\frac{1}{16}$ green wrinkled

If a $YyWw$ hybrid is self-pollinated, and eight seeds are produced, what is the probability of obtaining four green wrinkled seeds among these eight? _____

The probability of getting a green wrinkled plant is a or $\frac{1}{16}$ and the probability of getting anything else is b or $\frac{15}{16}$. Expand the binomial $(a + b)^8$ to get
$a^8 + 8a^7b + 28a^6b^2 + 56a^5b^3 + 70a^4b^4 + 56a^3b^5 + 28a^2b^6 + 8ab^7 + b^8$.

The term to use is $70a^4b^4$. Substituting,
$70a^4b^4 = 70 \times (\frac{1}{16})^4 \times (\frac{15}{16})^4 =$

$70 \times \frac{1}{16} \times \frac{1}{16} \times \frac{1}{16} \times \frac{1}{16} \times \frac{15}{16} \times \frac{15}{16} \times \frac{15}{16} \times \frac{15}{16} = \frac{3,543,750}{4,294,967,296} = $ about $\frac{1}{1,212}$.

*Progress Quiz II. B: Using the Binomial Expansion Principle
in Calculating Probabilities*

When you have completed this quiz, check your answers against
those provided in Appendix B at the end of this book.

1.   a.   The expansion of the binomial $(a + b)^N$ can be used in
calculating probabilities when the two terms of the binomial are
probability values, the sum of which is _____ .

b.   The exponent, N, represents _____ .

2.   In a litter of nine kittens, what is the probability of having
four males and five females in any order? _____

3.   In the previous problem you saw that there are 126 different
orders in which one can obtain a litter of nine kittens consisting
of four males and five females. One of the 126 possible orders is
to have four males born followed by five females. Now, in a litter
of nine kittens, what is the probability of getting four males and
five females *in that order?* _____

4. In shorthorn cattle, R represents the gene for red coat color and r represents the gene for white coat color. If an individual is heterozygous, Rr, both genes are expressed, resulting in a roan coat color. If a roan male is crossed with a roan female, the expected results are:

$\frac{1}{4}$ of offspring RR—red coat color

$\frac{1}{2}$ of offspring Rr—roan coat color

$\frac{1}{4}$ of offspring rr—white coat color

Five such matings of roan cattle were made, and five offspring were produced.

a. What is the probability that, among these five offspring, four will be red and one will be either roan or white (non-red)? _____

b. What is the probability that, among these five offspring, three will be red and two will be either roan or white? _____

5. Suppose that an Aa female is mated to an Aa male and four progeny are produced. What is the probability that in this family of four offspring there will be a perfect Mendelian ratio of $3A\_$ to $1aa$? _____

III
THE
CHI-SQUARE
TEST

Performance Objectives

As a result of conscientious study of this chapter, you will be able to

- state the formula for calculating the statistic, chi-square;

- calculate the expected number of individuals in each category, given the anticipated ratio in which the various categories are expected to occur;

- calculate the deviations between observed and expected numbers in each category;

- calculate the statistic, chi-square;

- use a chi-square table to determine the probability that deviations between observed and expected numbers are due to chance alone;

- apply the chi-square test to determining the "goodness of fit" of experimentally obtained biological data to a hypothesized ratio.

104. What is the chi-square test and when is it used? Up to this time we have assumed that the deviations from predicted results were due to chance alone. However, there are times when they are *not* due to chance.

Chi-square is a statistical test or procedure in which observed results are compared with theoretical expectations to determine whether the observed deviations from predicted results are due to chance alone or some other factor. For example, if matings of female mice with males of a particular strain resulted in what appeared to be abnormally large numbers of female offspring, one might reasonably question whether or not these results were due to chance alone. By use of the chi-square test to compare the observed results (number of female vs. number of male offspring) with the expected results (one would expect half of the offspring to be males and half to be females), one could determine the probability of the observed deviations occurring due to chance alone. In other words, chi-square is a test used to determine the probability that observed data are an example of a particular hypothesized result.

To summarize, the chi-square test may be used when we wish to determine whether observed deviations from expected results are due to _____ alone or to some other factor.

---

chance

105. X is the Greek letter *chi* and is the symbol used to represent a particular statistical test. Therefore, X^2 stands for _____ .

---

chi-square

106. Whenever you determine X^2, you will always have at least two terms because there will be at least two alternatives that could have been observed—heads or tails; boys or girls; red, roan or white cattle; yellow round, yellow wrinkled, green round or green wrinkled peas.

The X^2 value is determined by using the following equations:

$$X^2 = \Sigma \frac{(O - E)^2}{E}$$

In this equation, the Greek letter sigma, Σ, means *the sum of all,* O represents the observed results and E represents the corresponding expected results.

a.   From the equation above, $(O - E)$ means _____.
_____.

b.   The superscript $(^2)$ means _____
_____ .

---

a. $(O - E)$ means the observed results minus the corresponding expected results, the deviations.

b.   The superscript $(^2)$ indicates that this value $(O - E)$ is to be squared or multiplied by itself.

107. X^2 problems will have different numbers of terms, depending on the number of possible results. One less than the number of possible results is called the number of degrees of freedom. For example, in matings of guinea pigs heterozygous for black coat color (carrying the recessive gene for white), the number of possible results are two—black and white. Those guinea pigs which are not black will be white. Therefore, the number of degrees of freedom here is _____ .

one

> *Problem I.* (Use this problem for answering frames
> 108-113.) A coin is tossed 100 times and it is observed
> that 60 times it lands with heads up and 40 times with
> tails up.

108. From the 100 tosses, you would expect (a.)_____ heads
and (b.)_____ tails.

This is a 1:1 ratio.

You know from previous work that you can expect heads $\frac{1}{2}$ of
the time and tails $\frac{1}{2}$ of the time. From 100 tosses this would be
(a.) 50 heads and (b.) 50 tails.

109. In setting up the X^2 test, we will use the observed number
of heads minus the expected number of heads to calculate the
first term. Likewise, the observed number of tails minus the
expected number of tails is used to calculate the second term.

Now, substitute the values given in Problem I and frame 108 into
the equations below.

a.   For the first term:

$$\frac{(\text{observed no. of heads} - \text{expected no. of heads})^2}{\text{expected no. of heads}} = \frac{(\qquad)^2}{(\qquad)}$$

b.   For the second term:

$$\frac{(\text{observed no. of tails} - \text{expected no. of tails})^2}{\text{expected no. of tails}} = \frac{(\qquad)^2}{(\qquad)}$$

a. For the first term: $\dfrac{(60-50)^2}{50}$

b. For the second term: $\dfrac{(40-50)^2}{50}$

110. Now, substitute these data into the χ^2 equation.

For this problem:

$$\chi^2 = \Sigma\ \frac{(O-E)^2}{E} = \text{first term} + \text{second term}$$

$$\chi^2 = \underline{\hspace{3cm}} + \underline{\hspace{3cm}}$$

$$\chi^2 = \frac{(60-50)^2}{50} + \frac{(40-50)^2}{50}$$

111. Using the answer to frame 110, complete the calculation of χ^2. (In calculating χ^2 values, carry your calculations to three decimal places.) $\chi^2 = \underline{\hspace{2cm}}$

$$\chi^2 = \Sigma \, \frac{(O - E)^2}{E}$$

$$= \frac{(60 - 50)^2}{50} + \frac{(40 - 50)^2}{50}$$

$$= \frac{(10)^2}{50} + \frac{(-10)^2}{50}$$

$$= \frac{100}{50} + \frac{100}{50}$$

$$= 2 + 2$$

$$= 4$$

112. How many degrees of freedom do you have in interpreting the χ^2 value you have just calculated? _____

There are two terms in the χ^2 calculation since there are two possible results, heads or tails. Therefore, there is one degree of freedom (i.e., one less than the number of possible results).

113. When solving chi-square problems, we will employ a table found in Appendix A to determine whether the calculated chi-square value is sufficiently small for the deviations to be attributed to chance alone. Now turn to page 111 and read the directions for using the Table of Chi-Square Values.

Using the χ^2 value of 4 (which you calculated in frame 111) and remembering that for this problem there is one degree of freedom (frame 112), locate the number 1 in the degrees of freedom (n) column. Go across from the n = 1 until you come to 3.841 and 5.412. The calculated χ^2 value of 4 lies between these two values.

Chi-square is arbitrarily considered to be statistically significant when the probability is less than 5%. The value, 4, is greater than 3.841, the value above which χ^2 becomes statistically significant when there are two terms (or one degree of freedom). Therefore, it is likely that some factor other than chance was operating in this case.

In other words, the probability is that our observed deviations are:

a.   too (large/small) _____ and
b.   (may/may not) _____ be attributed to chance alone.

---

a.   large
b.   may not

> *Problem II.* (Use this problem for answering frames 114-120.) A coin is tossed a total of ten times; seven times it lands heads, and three times, tails.

114. What is the expected ratio of heads to tails? _____

The expected ratio is 1:1.

115.   Using the expected ratio,

a.   What is the expected number of heads? _____
b.   Tails? _____

a.   Five.
b.   Five.

116. How many degrees of freedom are there in interpreting the χ^2 in this example? _____

There is one degree of freedom.

117. Calculate the χ^2 value for Problem II. $\chi^2 =$ _____

$$\chi^2 = \frac{(O - E)^2}{E} \quad + \quad \frac{(O - E)^2}{E}$$

$$= \frac{(7 - 5)^2}{5} \quad + \quad \frac{(3 - 5)^2}{5}$$

$$= \frac{(2)^2}{5} \quad + \quad \frac{(-2)^2}{5}$$

$$= \frac{4}{5} \quad + \quad \frac{4}{5}$$

$$= \frac{8}{5}$$

$$= 1.6$$

118. For Problem II, what is the maximum value that we could have for χ^2 and continue to attribute the observed deviations to chance? (See Table of Chi-Square Values, Appendix A.)

If the value for χ^2 is 3.841 or more we could *not* attribute the deviations to chance alone.

119. a.   On the basis of the calculations made in frame 117 and your answer for frame 118, are you now willing to accept the data (seven heads, three tails) as a satisfactory approximation of the predicted 1:1 ratio? _____
b.   In addition, are the deviations of the observed from the expected sufficiently small that they may be attributed to chance alone? _____

---

a.   Yes. From the table in Appendix A, we see that our calculated χ^2 value of 1.6 is considerably less than the maximum allowable value of 3.841, which is associated with the probability of 5% or one chance in 20. Therefore, the data *can be accepted* as a satisfactory approximation of the expected 1:1 ratio.
b.   Yes. The deviations observed in this experiment *can be attributed to chance alone.*

120. The χ^2 table in Appendix A can be used to obtain a more precise answer as to the probability that the deviations observed are attributable to chance alone. For example, we calculated χ^2 to be 1.6 in Problem II, above. We have noted that we have one degree of freedom in interpreting this χ^2.

Look at the one-degree-of-freedom row in the table. The value

1.6 lies between the values 1.074 and 1.642. These X^2 values are found in the .30 and .20 probability columns, respectively. In fact, the value of 1.6 is very close to the value (1.642) in the .20 column. This means that the probability that the deviations observed in this problem are due to chance is approximately 20%. In other words, if this experiment were done repeatedly, you might expect to observe deviations as large or larger than the ones actually observed in approximately 20% of the trials.

Given a X^2 value of 1.325 in a situation in which you have three degrees of freedom,

a. What table values of X^2 lie on either side of the given X^2 value (1.325)? _____

b. What is the probability that the deviations (upon which this X^2 value of 1.325 was calculated) are due to chance alone?

_____

a. 1.005 and 1.424

b. The probability that the deviations are due to chance alone is between 70% and 80%.

> *Problem III.* (Use this problem for answering frames 121-124.) A garden pea seed is planted. It is heterozygous for the alleles concerning seed shape, round (W) versus wrinkled (w). This plant was self-pollinated and 26 round and six wrinkled seeds were obtained from it.

121. If these data were deviations from a 3:1 ratio, the *expected* number of round and wrinkled seeds would be (a.) _____ round and (b.) _____ wrinkled seeds.

The total number of seeds was 32. The expected results would be

a. $\frac{3}{4}$ X 32 = 24 round and

b. $\frac{1}{4}$ X 32 = 8 wrinkled seeds, for a perfect 3:1 ratio.

122. How many degrees of freedom are there in the interpretation of X^2 in this problem? _____

One degree of freedom.

123. Calculate X^2 for the Problem III data. The X^2 value = _____ .

$$X^2 = \frac{(O - E)^2}{E} + \frac{(O - E)^2}{E}$$

$$= \frac{(26 - 24)^2}{24} + \frac{(6 - 8)^2}{8}$$

$$= \frac{(2)^2}{24} + \frac{(-2)^2}{8}$$

$$= \frac{4}{24} + \frac{4}{8}$$

$$= \frac{4}{24} + \frac{12}{24}$$

$$= \frac{16}{24}$$

$$= 0.667$$

124. Look up this X^2 value of 0.667 in the table in Appendix A and complete the following:

a.   What table values of X^2 lie on either side of the calculated value, 0.667?_____ and _____

b.   What is the approximate probability that the observed deviations are due to chance alone? _____

c.   Are you willing to accept the data as a satisfactory approximation of a 3:1 ratio? _____

d.   Is it reasonable to conclude that the deviations are due to chance alone? _____

---

a.   0.455 and 1.074
b.   The probability lies between 30% and 50%.
c.   Yes.
d.   Yes.

> *Problem IV.* (Use this problem for answering frames 125-130.) In shorthorn cattle, individuals heterozygous for the alleles R and r (which determine the coat color) are mated. The observed results of 200 calves from approximately 200 such matings were 106 roan, 40 white and 54 red calves.

125. From a cross such as the above, what phenotypic ratio would you expect? _____

The expected ratio is one red animal to two roan animals to one white animal, or a 1:2:1 ratio.

126. How many red, roan and white animals would be expected in the 200-calf sample? _____ red; _____ roan; _____ white

From 200 animals, one would expect 50 red, 100 roan and 50 white.

127. In this problem, how many degrees of freedom are there in interpreting X^2? _____

There are three phenotypes (red, roan and white) and there will be three terms in the X^2 test; therefore, there are two degrees of freedom.

128. Calculate X^2 for the data in this problem. $X^2 = $ _____

$$\chi^2 = \frac{(O - E)^2}{E} + \frac{(O - E)^2}{E} + \frac{(O - E)^2}{E}$$

$$= \frac{(54 - 50)^2}{50} + \frac{(106 - 100)^2}{100} + \frac{(40 - 50)^2}{50}$$

$$= \frac{(4)^2}{50} + \frac{(6)^2}{100} + \frac{(-10)^2}{50}$$

$$= \frac{16}{50} + \frac{36}{100} + \frac{100}{50}$$

$$= \frac{32}{100} + \frac{36}{100} + \frac{200}{100}$$

$$= \frac{268}{100}$$

$$= 2.68$$

129. In this problem, what is the maximum χ^2 value if the observed deviations are to be attributed to chance? _____

The maximum χ^2 value, with two degrees of freedom, is 5.991. That is, if $\chi^2 = 5.991$, the probability is 5% that deviations are due to chance.

130. On the basis of the calculations made in frame 128, and your answer for frame 129, are you now willing to accept the data (40 white, 106 roan, 54 red) as a satisfactory approximation of the predicted 1:2:1 ratio? _____

The probability that the deviations observed are due to chance alone is between 20% and 30% since our calculated X^2 of 2.68 lies between 2.408 (30% column) and 3.219 (20% column). Therefore, yes, the data are satisfactory.

Problem V. (Use this problem for answering frames 131-135.) Two pea plants, each heterozygous for color of seeds and texture of seeds, are crossed. We expect to get a phenotypic ratio of nine yellow round seeds to three yellow wrinkled to three green round to one green wrinkled (9:3:3:1 ratio). From a cross like the one described above, 336 seeds were collected. There were 189 yellow round, 50 yellow wrinkled, 69 green round and 28 green wrinkled seeds.

---

131. Using the $\frac{9}{16}$, $\frac{3}{16}$, $\frac{3}{16}$, $\frac{1}{16}$ probability distribution, calculate the expected numbers of each type of seed.

a. _____ yellow round
b. _____ yellow wrinkled
c. _____ green round
d. _____ green wrinkled

The expected numbers of each type of seed are as follows:

a. $\frac{9}{16}$ of 336 seeds = 189 yellow round
b. $\frac{3}{16}$ of 336 seeds = 63 yellow wrinkled
c. $\frac{3}{16}$ of 336 seeds = 63 green round
d. $\frac{1}{16}$ of 336 seeds = 21 green wrinkled

132. How many degrees of freedom are there in interpreting the χ^2 for this problem? _____

There are three degrees of freedom.

133. Calculate χ^2 for the data in this problem. $\chi^2 =$ _____

$$\chi^2 = \frac{(189-189)^2}{189} + \frac{(50-63)^2}{63} + \frac{(69-63)^2}{63} + \frac{(28-21)^2}{21}$$

$$= \frac{(0)^2}{189} + \frac{(-13)^2}{63} + \frac{(6)^2}{63} + \frac{(7)^2}{21}$$

$$= 0 + \frac{169}{63} + \frac{36}{63} + \frac{49}{21}$$

$$= 0 + \frac{169}{63} + \frac{36}{63} + \frac{147}{63}$$

$$= \frac{352}{63}$$

$$= 5.587$$

134. In this problem, what is the maximum X^2 value if the observed deviations are to be attributed to chance? _____

The maximum X^2 value, with three degrees of freedom, is 7.816.

135. On the basis of the calculation made in frame 133, and your answer for frame 134, are you now willing to accept the data (189 yellow round, 50 yellow wrinkled, 69 green round, 28 green wrinkled) as a satisfactory approximation of the predicted 9:3:3:1 ratio? _____

The probability that the deviations observed are due to chance alone is between 10% and 20% since our calculated X^2 of 5.587 lies between 4.642 (20% column) and 6.251 (10% column). Therefore, the data are acceptable.

Progress Quiz III: The Chi-Square Test

When you have completed this quiz, check your answers against those provided in Appendix B at the end of this book.

1. When and why is the chi-square test used?

2. a. Write the equation for X^2. _____
  b. The Greek letter sigma (Σ) means _____ .
  c. The O stands for the _____ .
  d. The E stands for the _____ .
  e. The value (O − E) is called the _____ .
  f. The superscript (^{2}) means _____ .

3. In a family of six children, would five girls and one boy be a reasonable approximation of the expected ratio? To answer this question, answer the following:

a. What is the expected ratio? _____
b. What must you do to determine whether a family of five girls and one boy is a satisfactory approximation of the expected ratio?

_____

c. Is a family of five girls and one boy a good fit to the ratio?

_____

4.   Remember that albinism in man is due to a recessive gene. If a couple, both heterozygous for this particular gene, have eight children, we would expect the following phenotypic results:

a. _____ normal and _____ albino children.
b.   This would represent a _____ ratio.

5.   From a situation similar to the one described in frame 4, would four normal children and four albino children constitute a reasonable approximation of the expected results? _____
How do you know? _____

6.   If a pure black Andalusian chicken is crossed with a splashed white Andalusian (white with black splashes), the resulting off-spring are called *blue*. If two of these blue individuals are mated, we expect one black, two blue and one white offspring (1:2:1). It appears that this ratio occurs in much the same way that red, roan and white coat colors occur in shorthorn cattle. If blue chickens are mated and, among 600 offspring, 180 black, 190 white and 230 blue chickens are observed, would one be justified in attributing the observed deviations to chance alone? _____
How do you know? _____

7.   If two guinea pigs, each heterozygous for coat color, are mated, do 195 black and 85 white offspring approximate the ratio expected from such a cross? _____ How do you know?_____

> *Problem VI.* (Use for answering frames 8-13.) Let *A* represent the gene for one trait and *B* represent the gene for a second trait. Two organisms, each hetero-zygous for traits *A* and *B*, are crossed. The following results are obtained: 384 *A__B__*, 123 *A__bb*, 130 *aaB__* and 35 *aabb*.

8. What is the expected ratio for these data? _____

9. Using the expected ratio from frame 8, how many of each type of offspring would one expect?

a. _____ *A__B__*
b. _____ *A__bb*
c. _____ *aaB__*
d. _____ *aabb*

10. If you calculate X^2 for Problem VI, how many degrees of freedom will you have in interpreting the X^2? _____.

11. Calculate X^2 for the data in Problem VI. The value of X^2 is _____ .

12. What is the probability that the deviations are due to chance in this problem? _____

13. Do the results observed approximate the expected ratio?

_____

IV
COMPREHENSIVE
REVIEW

If you have difficulty with particular frames in this review, re-study the related frames indicated. *You must be able to work the problems in this review if you are to pass the final examination, which covers material from the entire program.* The objective of this chapter is that you be able to apply and practice all the skills you have obtained in Chapters I, II and III.

136. In a family consisting of two children,

a.　How many possible combinations or orders of birth for boys and girls are there? _____
b.　What are these possible combinations? _____

a.	First Child		Second Child		Total Possible Combinations of Boys and Girls
	2 possibilities (boy or girl)	X	2 possibilities (boy or girl)	=	4
b.	B		B		BB
	B		G		BG
	G		B		GB
	G		G		GG

If you missed this frame, review frames 3-24.

137. There are ten specimens of deciduous trees in a small wooded lot. Each of the ten represents a different species. A botany student is instructed to obtain three specimens from this lot, each specimen representing a *different* species. How many possible combinations of three different species can be made from the ten species growing in the lot? _____

He has ten choices for his first specimen. Once he has selected his first specimen, he has only nine different species from which to choose his second specimen. Likewise, once he has selected his second specimen, he has only eight different species from which to choose the third specimen. Therefore, he has a total of 10 X 9 X 8 or 720 possible combinations.

If you missed this frame, review frames 44-46 and 56.

138. A plant having the genotype *AaBb* is crossed with one having the same genotype (*AaBb*). How many *different* possible combinations are there for the offspring of such a cross? _____

There are four gametic possibilities for each of the parent organisms: *AB, Ab, aB* and *ab*. Therefore, the total number of combinations for the offspring is 4 X 4 or 16.

	AB	Ab	aB	ab
AB	AABB	AAbB	aABB	aAbB
Ab	AABb	AAbb	aABb	aAbb
aB	AaBB	AabB	aaBB	aabB
ab	AaBb	Aabb	aaBb	aabb

However, note that not *all* of the possible combinations are different; there are, in fact, nine *different* possible genotypes. For example, *aAbB* is really the same genotype as *aABb* or *AabB* or *AaBb*.

If you missed this frame, review frames 3-24.

139. In a family of three children,

a.   What is the probability that a couple's first child will be a boy? _____
b.   What is the probability that, in a family of three children, all three will be boys? _____

---

a.   There are two possibilities, a boy or a girl. Therefore, the probability of the first child being a boy is one chance out of two possibilities or $\frac{1}{2}$.

b.   Here, the important thing to remember is that each child is a *separate* and *independent* event and the probability for a boy is $\frac{1}{2}$ each time. Therefore, the probability that all three children will be boys $= (\frac{1}{2})^3 = \frac{1}{2} \times \frac{1}{2} \times \frac{1}{2} = \frac{1}{8}$. (Also, there is an equal probability of having three girls.)

If you missed this frame, review frames 25-43.

140. What is the probability that a couple's first child will be either a boy or a girl? _____

The probability of a boy plus the probability of a girl $= \frac{1}{2} + \frac{1}{2} = 1$.

If you missed this frame, review frames 49-57.

141. The probability of an albino being born to parents heterozygous for this trait is $\frac{1}{4}$. What is the probability of such parents having three albino girls? _____

Probability of an Albino		Probability of a Girl		Probability of an Albino Girl
$\frac{1}{4}$	X	$\frac{1}{2}$	=	$\frac{1}{8}$

Probability of First Child Being an Albino Girl		Probability of Second Child Being an Albino Girl		Probability of Third Child Being an Albino Girl		Probability of Three Albino Girls
$\frac{1}{8}$	X	$\frac{1}{8}$	X	$\frac{1}{8}$	=	$\frac{1}{512}$

If you missed this frame, review frames 25-43.

142. In a particular family, the probability of having a child with type AB blood is $\frac{1}{4}$.

a.   What is the probability of having a *son* with type AB blood? _____

b.   What is the probability of having a *son* with any other blood type? _____

c.   What is the probability of having a *son*, and his having either type AB blood or any other type blood? _____

a.

Probability of AB blood		Probability of a Boy		Probability of a Boy with AB Blood
$\frac{1}{4}$	X	$\frac{1}{2}$	=	$\frac{1}{8}$

b.

Probability of Any Other Type Blood		Probability of a Boy		Probability of a Boy with Any Other Type Blood
$\frac{3}{4}$	X	$\frac{1}{2}$	=	$\frac{3}{8}$

c.

Probability of a Boy with AB Blood		Probability of a Boy with Any Other Type Blood		Probability of a Boy with Either AB or Any Other Blood Type
$\frac{1}{8}$	+	$\frac{3}{8}$	=	$\frac{4}{8}$ or $\frac{1}{2}$

If you missed this frame, review frames 56-60.

143. Indicate what each part of the binomial $(a + b)^N$ means.

The *a* is the probability of one event occurring.
The *b* is the probability of an alternative event occurring (note that $a + b = 1$).
N equals the total number of events being considered.

If you missed this frame, review frame 71.

144. Expand the binomial $(a + b)^4$. The product obtained is:

$(a + b)^4 = a^4 + 4a^3b + 6a^2b^2 + 4ab^3 + b^4.$

If you missed this frame, review frames 71-78.

145. One of the terms from the expanded binomial $(a + b)^4$ is $6a^2b^2$. Indicate how each part of this term may be interpreted.

$6a^2b^2$

The a is the probability of one event occurring; the exponent (^{2}) refers to the event occurring twice (for which a represents the probability). The b is the probability of an alternative event occurring; the exponent (^{2}) refers to the event occurring twice (for which b represents the probability). The coefficient (6) means there are six possible orders in which the one event can occur twice and the alternative event can occur twice.

If you missed this frame, review frames 81-87.

146. In a family consisting of four children, what is the probability of three girls and one boy in any order? _____

By binomial expansion, $(a + b)^4 = a^4 + 4a^3b + 6a^2b^2 + 4ab^3 + b^4$. The term we use to determine the probability of three girls and one boy in a family of four children is $4a^3b$. If we let a equal the probability of a girl $(\frac{1}{2})$ and b equal the probability of a boy $(\frac{1}{2})$, then $4a^3b = 4 \left(\frac{1}{2}\right)^3 \times \left(\frac{1}{2}\right) =$

$4 \left(\frac{1}{2}\right)^4 = 4 \times \frac{1}{2} \times \frac{1}{2} \times \frac{1}{2} \times \frac{1}{2} = \frac{4}{16} = \frac{1}{4} =$ the probability of a family of four children having three girls and one boy in any order.

If you missed this frame, review frames 61-98.

147. In a particular family, the probability of having a child with type AB blood is $\frac{1}{4}$. If this family consists of five children, what is the probability of having two children with type AB blood and three children with A, B or O blood? _____

Using binomial expansion, $(a + b)^5 =$
$a^5 + 5a^4b + 10a^3b^2 + 10a^2b^3 + 5ab^4 + b^5$. The term we use to determine the probability of two children with type AB blood and three children with A, B or O blood in a family of five children is $10a^2b^3$. If a is the probability of type AB blood ($\frac{1}{4}$) and b is the probability of A, B or O blood ($\frac{3}{4}$), and we have ten different orders in which we can have two children with type AB blood and three children with type A, B or O blood, then
$10a^2b^3 = 10(\frac{1}{4})^2 \times (\frac{3}{4})^3$

$= 10 \times \frac{1}{4} \times \frac{1}{4} \times \frac{3}{4} \times \frac{3}{4} \times \frac{3}{4}$

$= \frac{270}{1,024}$

$= \frac{135}{512}$ or about $\frac{1}{3.79}$

If you missed this frame, review frames 61-98.

148. When do you use the X^2 test?

When you want to determine whether deviations of observed results from the expected results are due to chance alone or to some other factor. (or comparable answer)

If you missed this frame, review frame 104.

149. Write the equation used for the chi-square test.

$$\chi^2 = \Sigma \ \frac{(O - E)^2}{E}$$

If you missed this frame, review frames 104-106.

150. In the χ^2 equation,

a.   Sigma (Σ) stands for _____ .
b.   The O stands for _____ .
c.   The E stands for _____ .
d.   The superscript (^{2}) means _____
_____ .

---

a. Σ stands for the sum of all values of $\frac{(O - E)^2}{E}$.

b. O stands for the observed results.
c. E stands for the expected results.
d.   The superscript (^{2}) means that the value inside the parentheses is to be squared.

If you missed this frame, review frames 104-106.

151. When the chi-square value obtained by using the formula is sufficiently small,

a.　We say the deviations from expected results are due to
_____ .

However, if the calculated chi-square value is sufficiently high,

b.　We say that chi-square becomes statistically significant, and it is likely that the deviations from expected results are due to
_____ .

---

a.　chance (or chance alone)
b.　some factor other than chance

If you missed this frame, review frames 104-113 and Appendix A.

152. (Use the Table of Chi-Square Values in Appendix A for this frame.) For one degree of freedom, X^2 becomes statistically significant when the X^2 value exceeds _____ .

3.841

If you missed this frame, review frames 113 and 118 and Appendix A.

153. When the calculated X^2 value is 3.841 (with one degree of freedom), the *probability* that the deviations are due to chance alone is _____ .

5% (or five chances out of 100 or one chance in 20)

If you missed this frame, review frames 118-120 and Appendix A.

154. Shorthorn cattle heterozygous for the alleles R and r are mated. The 1,000 calves produced from approximately 1,000 such matings include 540 roan, 250 red and 210 white calves.

a.   Calculate X^2 for the data in this problem. _____
b.   Using your calculated X^2 value and the Table of Chi-Square Values in Appendix A, are the deviations from the expected results due to chance alone? _____

---

a. X^2 $=$ $\Sigma \dfrac{(O-E)^2}{E}$

$$= \dfrac{(O-E)^2}{E} + \dfrac{(O-E)^2}{E} + \dfrac{(O-E)^2}{E}$$

$$= \dfrac{(250-250)^2}{250} + \dfrac{(540-500)^2}{500} + \dfrac{(210-250)^2}{250}$$

$$= 0 + \dfrac{(40)^2}{500} + \dfrac{(-40)^2}{250}$$

$$= 0 + \dfrac{1,600}{500} + \dfrac{1,600}{250}$$

$$= 0 + \dfrac{1,600}{500} + \dfrac{1,200}{500}$$

$$= \dfrac{4,800}{500}$$

$$= 9.6$$

b.   No.

If you missed this frame, review frames 104-135.

155. Using the Table of Chi-Square Values in Appendix A, what is the *probability* that the deviations observed in frame 154 are due to chance alone? _____

The probability is less than 1% that such deviations are due to chance alone.

If you missed this frame, review frames 104-135.

Appendix A

How to Use the Table of Chi-Square Values

1. Solve the X^2 problem to determine what the X^2 value is. For example, assume that $X^2 = 0.159$.
2. Determine the number of degrees of freedom and find that number in the first column on the left. For example, let us use n = 1.
3. Go across from n = 1 until you come to 0.148. The X^2 value, 0.159, lies between 0.148 and 0.455. Look up to the top row for the probability values; the observed deviations would be expected between 50% and 70% of the time due to chance alone. Therefore, X^2 is *not* statistically significant and the deviations *can* be attributed to chance.
4. X^2 is arbitrarily considered to be statistically significant when P is *less* than 5%; that is, when the probability that the deviations are due to chance alone is less than one chance in 20. When P is less than 5%, you can conclude that it is improbable that the deviations are due to chance alone. A probability (P) value of less than 1% is regarded as highly significant and you can conclude that it is highly improbable that the deviations are due to chance alone.

Table of Chi-Square Values: (Abridged from Table III of Fisher and Yates: *Statistical Tables for Biological, Agricultural and Medical Research,* published by Oliver and Boyd, Ltd. Edinburgh, and by permission of the authors and publishers.)

n	P / .99	.98	.95	.90	.80	.70	.50	.30	.20	.10	.05	.02	.01
1	.000157	.000628	.00393	.0158	.0642	.148	.455	1.074	1.642	2.706	3.841	5.412	6.635
2	.0201	.0404	.103	.211	.446	.713	1.386	2.408	3.219	4.605	5.991	7.824	9.210
3	.115	.185	.352	.584	1.005	1.424	2.366	3.665	4.642	6.251	7.816	9.837	11.345
4	.297	.429	.711	1.064	1.649	2.195	3.357	4.878	5.989	7.779	9.488	11.668	13.277
5	.554	.752	1.145	1.610	2.343	3.000	4.351	6.064	7.289	9.236	11.070	13.388	15.086
6	.872	1.134	1.635	2.204	3.070	3.828	5.348	7.231	8.558	10.645	12.592	15.033	16.812
7	1.239	1.564	2.167	2.833	3.822	4.671	6.346	8.383	9.803	12.017	14.067	16.622	18.475
8	1.646	2.032	2.733	3.490	4.594	5.527	7.344	9.524	11.030	13.362	15.507	18.168	20.090
9	2.088	2.532	3.325	4.168	5.380	6.393	8.343	10.656	12.242	14.684	16.919	19.679	21.666
10	2.558	3.059	3.940	4.865	6.179	7.267	9.342	11.781	13.442	15.987	18.307	21.161	23.209

Key for symbols used in this table:

n = the number of degrees of freedom, 1 through 10 in the first column

P = the probability of the deviations being due to chance alone; these values are in the top row. P can be read as a percentage by moving the decimal two places to the right.

χ^2 values = all of the other columns of numbers

Appendix B

I.   *Basic Probability Principles*

1. $2 \times 2 \times 2 = 8$
2. $10 \times 10 = 100$
3. $\frac{1}{4} \times \frac{1}{2} = \frac{1}{8}$
4. $\frac{1}{2} \times \frac{1}{2} = \frac{1}{4}$
5. $\frac{1}{6} + \frac{1}{6} = \frac{2}{6} = \frac{1}{3}$
6. $\frac{1}{5} + \frac{2}{5} = \frac{3}{5}$
7.   a. plus;   b. times
8.   a. $\frac{1}{2} \times \frac{1}{2} = \frac{1}{4}$;   b. $\frac{1}{2} \times \frac{1}{2} = \frac{1}{4}$;
     c. $\frac{1}{2} \times \frac{1}{2} = \frac{1}{4}$;   d. $\frac{1}{2} \times \frac{1}{2} = \frac{1}{4}$;
     e. $\frac{1}{4} + \frac{1}{4} = \frac{1}{2}$;   f. $\frac{1}{4} + \frac{1}{4} + \frac{1}{4} + \frac{1}{4} = 1$
9. $(\frac{1}{4} \times \frac{1}{4} \times \frac{1}{4}) + (\frac{1}{4} \times \frac{1}{4} \times \frac{1}{4}) = \frac{1}{64} + \frac{1}{64} = \frac{2}{64} = \frac{1}{32}$
10. a. $\frac{4}{19}$;   b. $\frac{5}{19}$;   c. $\frac{5}{19} + \frac{5}{19} + \frac{5}{19} = \frac{15}{19}$;
     d. $\frac{3}{18} = \frac{1}{6}$;   e. $\frac{5}{20} \times \frac{4}{19} \times \frac{3}{18} = \frac{1}{4} \times \frac{4}{19} \times \frac{1}{6} = \frac{1}{114}$

II. A. *Expanding the Binomial*

1.   third
2. $(a + b)^3 = a^3 + 3a^2b + 3ab^2 + b^3$; the term is $3ab^2$
3.   a.   fifth; a; b

b. three

c. b; the number of times the event having probability b occurs

d. number

4. $a^7 + a^6b + a^5b^2 + a^4b^3 + a^3b^4 + a^2b^5 + ab^6 + b^7$

5. $a^7 + 7a^6b + 21a^5b^2 + 35a^4b^3 + 35a^3b^4 + 21a^2b^5 + 7ab^6 + b^7$

6. a. $35a^4b^3 = 35(\frac{1}{2})^4(\frac{1}{2})^3 = \dfrac{35}{128}$

   b. $b^7 = (\frac{1}{2})^7 = \dfrac{1}{128}$

II. B. *Using the Binomial Expansion Principle in Calculating Probabilities*

1. a. 1

   b. the total number of events (or individuals) being considered

2. $(a + b)^9 = a^9 + 9a^8b + 36a^7b^2 + 84a^6b^3 + 126a^5b^4 + 126a^4b^5$ etc.

   $126a^4b^5$ is the term to use

   $126 (\frac{1}{2})^4(\frac{1}{2})^5 = \dfrac{126}{(2\times2\times2\times2)\ (2\times2\times2\times2\times2)} = \dfrac{63}{256}$

3. $(\frac{1}{2}\times\frac{1}{2}\times\frac{1}{2}\times\frac{1}{2})\ (\frac{1}{2}\times\frac{1}{2}\times\frac{1}{2}\times\frac{1}{2}\times\frac{1}{2}) = \dfrac{1}{16} \times \dfrac{1}{32} = \dfrac{1}{512}$

4. probability of red = a = $\frac{1}{4}$

   probability of roan or white = b = $\frac{3}{4}$

   $(a + b)^5 = a^5 + 5a^4b + 10a^3b^2$ etc.

   a. $5a^4b = 5 (\frac{1}{4})^4 (\frac{3}{4}) = \dfrac{15}{1,024}$

   b. $10a^3b^2 = 10 (\frac{1}{4})^3(\frac{3}{4})^2 = \dfrac{90}{1,024} = \dfrac{45}{512}$

5. $(a + b)^4 = a^4 + 4a^3b$ etc.

   a = probability of $A\_$ phenotype = $\frac{3}{4}$

   b = probability of aa phenotype = $\frac{1}{4}$

$4 a^3 b = 4 (\frac{3}{4})^3 (\frac{1}{4}) = \frac{27}{64}$, meaning that in a family of only four children where a 3:1 ratio is expected, the probability of getting that 3:1 ratio is less than 50% ($\frac{27}{64}$, to be exact). This is why geneticists prefer to work with organisms producing large numbers of progeny so that the probability of getting an expected ratio will be higher.

III. *The Chi-Square Test*

1. Chi-square is employed when we wish to determine whether data observed in a particular experiment are a satisfactory approximation to a particular hypothesized ratio.

2. a. $\chi^2 = \Sigma \dfrac{(O - E)^2}{E}$

b. sum of (all possible values)
c. observed values
d. corresponding expected values
e. deviation
f. square, that is, the item multiplied by itself

3. a. 1:1
b. Calculate χ^2 and determine whether the probability is greater than 5% that the deviations are due to chance alone.
c. Yes, as can be seen from the following calculations:

	O	E	O–E	$(O-E)^2$	$\dfrac{(O-E)^2}{E}$
Females	5	3	2	4	$\frac{4}{3}$
Males	1	3	–2	4	$\frac{4}{3}$
	6				$\chi^2 = \frac{8}{3} = 2\frac{2}{3} = 2.67$

degree of freedom = 1; P = probability = about 10%

4. a. six normal and two albino; b. 3:1 ratio
5. Yes. By calculating χ^2 and determining the probability (P) value as shown below:

	O	E	O−E	$(O-E)^2$	$\dfrac{(O-E)^2}{E}$
Normal	4	6	−2	4	$\dfrac{4}{6}$
Albino	4	2	2	4	$\dfrac{4}{2}$
	$\overline{8}$				$\chi^2 = 2\frac{2}{3} = 2.67$

degree of freedom = 1; P = about 10%

6. No. By calculating χ^2 and determining that P is less than 5% as shown below:

	O	E	O−E	$(O-E)^2$	$\dfrac{(O-E)^2}{E}$
Black	180	150	30	900	$\dfrac{900}{150} = \dfrac{1,800}{300}$
Blue	230	300	−70	4,900	$\dfrac{4,900}{300} = \dfrac{4,900}{300}$
White	190	150	40	1,600	$\dfrac{1,600}{150} = \dfrac{3,200}{300}$
	$\overline{600}$				$\chi^2 = \dfrac{99}{3} = 33$

degrees of freedom = 2; P is less than 1%

7. No. By calculating χ^2 and determining that P is less than 5% as shown below:

	O	E	O−E	$(O-E)^2$	$\dfrac{(O-E)^2}{E}$
Black	195	210	−15	225	$\dfrac{225}{210} = \dfrac{225}{210}$
White	85	70	15	225	$\dfrac{225}{70} = \dfrac{675}{210}$
	$\overline{280}$				$\chi^2 = \dfrac{900}{210} = \dfrac{30}{7}$

degree of freedom = 1; P is less than 5% $\chi^2 = 4.2857$

8. 9:3:3:1
9. a. 378; b. 126; c. 126; d. 42
10. three
11.

	O	E	O−E	$(O-E)^2$	$\dfrac{(O-E)^2}{E}$
$A\_B\_$	384	378	6	36	$\dfrac{36}{378} = \dfrac{36}{378}$
A_bb	123	126	−3	9	$\dfrac{9}{126} = \dfrac{27}{378}$
$aaB\_$	130	126	4	16	$\dfrac{16}{126} = \dfrac{48}{378}$
$aabb$	35	42	−7	49	$\dfrac{49}{42} = \dfrac{441}{378}$
	672				$\chi^2 = \dfrac{552}{378} = 1.46$

12. $\chi^2 = 1.424$ for P = 70% (see Table, Appendix A); therefore, our χ^2 of 1.46 (frame 11) means that the probability is just under 70% that the deviations are due to chance alone.
13. Yes.

Bibliography

The references given below may serve as sources of supplemental reading for interested students using this program.

Bliss, C. I., *Statistics in Biology—Statistical Methods for Research in the Natural Sciences*, Vol. I. New York, McGraw-Hill Book Company, 1967.

Burns, George W., *The Science of Genetics*, 2nd. Ed. New York, The Macmillan Company, 1972.

Gardner, Eldon J., *Principles of Genetics*, 4th. Ed. New York, John Wiley and Sons, Inc., 1972.

Koosis, Donald J., *Statistics.* New York, John Wiley and Sons, Inc., 1972.

Lerner, I. Michael, *Heredity, Evolution and Society.* San Francisco, W. H. Freeman and Company, 1968.

Levine, Louis, *Biology of the Gene*, 2nd. Ed. Saint Louis, The C. V. Mosby Company, 1973.

Mosimann, James E., *Elementary Probability for the Biological Sciences.* New York, Appleton-Century-Crofts, 1968.

Srb, Adrian M., Owen, Ray D. and Edgar, Robert S., *General Genetics.* San Francisco, W. H. Freeman and Company, 1965.

Strickberger, Monroe W., *Genetics.* New York, The Macmillan Company, 1968.

Vann, Edwin, *Fundamentals of Biostatistics.* Lexington, Massachusetts, D. C. Heath and Company, 1972.

Winchester, A. M., *Genetics: A Survey of the Principles of Heredity*, 4th Ed. Boston, Houghton Mifflin Company, 1972.